# My Mother is Crazier than Your Mother

Cameron Castle

ISBN: 1495228614
ISBN 13: 9781495228612
Cover Design: Audrey Mackaman
Back Cover Photo: Michael Stadler
Cover Photo: My mother, feeling very much a golf widow, made a stuffed
replica of her third husband, Rudy, so while he was off playing another
late round of golf she didn't feel like she was dining alone.

This is a complete work of fiction ever since my mother turned 93. Before that, spot on.

Some names and descriptions have been reluctantly changed.

The author regrets the possibility that with this book he has limited his audience to only those who have, or have had mothers.

Dedicated to Mason Byford Taylor
Mase, you were amazing. I miss you.

# Author's note:

A word about the term "creative non-fiction." Many people believe it refers to fairly true stories that have been improved upon creatively so as to make them more interesting. Nothing could be further from the truth. Whoever came up with that horrible misnomer should be punished. I assume they were trying to differentiate between a book about the history of knitting, for example, and a memoir. It is not meant to imply anything in the memoir should be made up, but that a memoir, most likely, is not educational or historical, but merely entertaining. The word picked to describe that was *creative*.

Everything in this book is as true as I can get it. Some is corroborated by photos or multiple witnesses. Some is dependent upon my memory and how it compares to the memories of others. For example, way too much time was spent arguing with my mother and my sister over the color of our first Pontiac car. I vividly remember it as beige. They remember it as olive green. We have yet to find a picture of it, so three things come into play. My memory is way better than theirs, it is my book, and what the hell difference does it make? So, that car was beige.

That just illustrates the effort to be accurate. In different writing groups critiquing chapters of this book, there often were people who said, "Just change it. It will make it more interesting. What's wrong with that? It's creative non-fiction, remember?"

Why I wrote this book, why it is interesting and fun to me, is that everything in it happened. What makes it interesting is the fact that it's true.

My mother reviewed the chapter about her killing all of my and my siblings' pets. She called me immediately after finishing it and said,

"Trash! Pure fiction! What's wrong with you? If you want to tell that story I'll write it."

"Wow, Mom. What's wrong?"

"Taffeta bedspreads in the boy's bedroom? No mother in their right mind would have taffeta bedspreads in a boy's bedroom. I'll be a laughing stock. They were chenille!"

"I am so sorry, Mom. I'll fix it. I guess I don't even know what taffeta is."

"It is ruffle-y and shiny and feminine. How could you make such a mistake?"

"It's fixed. I'll change it. But what about the rest? You know, about killing all our pets?"

"Oh, that. That was spot on. Extraordinary, really. You have quite the knack. But, taffeta! You can't print that."

So, complete with a Pontiac that I am sure was beige, and bedspreads that beyond a shadow of a doubt were chenille, the following is the story of my mother. Oh, and she is crazier than your mother.

# Table of Contents

# Introduction

My mother broke onto a quarantined army base during World War II to see her husband, Truman, because, "I missed him." She made it past the circling searchlights and over a wire fence. She did it in her finest dress, pearls, and faux mink stole. They had only been married a short time, and, "Well, I missed him."

After sneaking on the night shift kitchen crew bus and convincing the driver to let her off before entering the base, she said the hardest part was timing the searchlight so she could climb over the fence. Questions I ask her about it are answered so matter-of-factly.

"Were there armed guards?"

"Yes. In the tower. They would have shot me if they saw me."

"How did you get over that fence?"

"I just had to time the light as it passed by. Then I just climbed over."

She made it over, ran to the first barracks, knocked, and surprised the hell out of the guy in green underwear opening the door. A good-looking woman all decked out, and wearing pearls, was by far the last thing he expected to see knocking on that door.

"Can you tell me where Truman Rose is sleeping?" she asked.

The guy had been sound asleep, so he just answered the question. "That second barracks over," and he pointed, like it was common to be awoken in the middle of the night on a quarantined army base by a beautiful woman.

She ran to that building and knocked on the door. Another sleepy soldier opened it.

"Is Truman Rose here?"

"Rose, somebody's here to see you."

Truman rushed to the door, staring at the only person on the planet who would, or could, pull off such a stunt, and fearing he would, only a month from becoming an officer, be washed out of the service on the spot if she was caught. He pulled her onto his cot and said, "How did you get in here?"

"I climbed over the fence," she said.

"Can you get out?"

"Yes."

"Be careful."

My mother said he was furious, and she left right away. Getting out was much harder because she wasn't as inspired as she was getting in. When Truman pulled her onto his cot she didn't know her string of pearls had broken. After she was gone, Truman had to do something with those pearls since he figured they might be a tad awkward to explain.

Later, after Truman was no longer quarantined, she took their allotment of rationed food stamps and spent the whole lot on one can of Valencia peaches. When he came home hungry and saw totally bare cupboards except for the can of peaches, horrified, he asked, though he knew the answer, "What happened at the store? Where is the food?"

"Well, I really wanted those peaches."

That was possibly the only other time Truman got mad at her.

Today, over the phone, my mother remembered that day as clear as if it happened this morning.

"The peaches were 31 points. A can of soup was two. He was so mad. Not only because it was a stupid thing to do, but there was only one fruit he didn't like. Peaches. Then, later, I put a new book of coupons in my brand new, blue leather purse that I never should have bought and left it on the bus. It only had a couple of bucks in it, but the coupon book was in it. I went back to retrieve it, but they said no one brought it in. So I said to Truman, 'You don't need to worry about me spending all our points on peaches, I lost the whole damn book.'"

Truman adored her. He looked like Errol Flynn, and they were in heaven together. Her quirkiness was all just part of the package he loved.

My mother has such glorious memories of her marriage to Truman Rose. He was a training pilot for the army, and they travelled around Texas and Southern California as he moved from base to base. They had a son they named Truman. When he was two-and-a-half, they had a second son, Steve. He was born in a hospital near Mom's family north of Chicago. Truman was in California flying training missions. In those days, after a C-section, mothers were allowed eight days to recover in the hospital.

Since Truman couldn't be there, he instructed Mom's Mom, Bessie, to each day deliver flowers and one of the poems he had written for her. But, on the sixth day, her mother came into the room with no roses and no poem. She had to deliver the news that Truman had died in a plane crash.

Truman's father and mother came to the hospital immediately to see the baby and help with my mom's grief. When Truman's father saw Steve he said, "This baby doesn't look right. He looks like he's failing. What are you doing about it? He needs a specialist. I want you to find the best doctor in the country and fly him in here. I will pay all the costs. I have just lost my son and I am not going to lose this baby."

They found a specialist in Salt Lake City, and flew him in. He arrived at 2:00 AM that evening. When he saw little Steve, he said, "This baby needs a blood transfusion immediately." Steve had an unusual blood type that the hospital didn't have. The pediatrician was there and said, "I have that blood type," and rolled up his sleeve. It worked, and Steve made it.

Losing her husband was the worst, but only one of many painful losses in her life. Thirty years after her loss of Truman, just she and I were living together in Glenview, Illinois. One afternoon she walked into the house, beaming. She had taken a test to measure one's stress level. Points were assigned for lost loved ones, lost loves, financial hardship, etc. She was very proud of her score. If a score of 300 meant likely to be depressed, and a score of 500 meant seek help, and a score of 700 meant danger, she was thrilled to death to bring in an 850.

She is spontaneous, impulsive, compulsive, excruciatingly meddlesome and an extravagant spendthrift. What she also is, is the kindest, most generous person you could meet. She is vivacious and bubbly, like a five year-old at the start of a birthday party. She is like that all the time. But her most important attribute is how she looks at the world; how she can come home thrilled with her record setting score on the stress test. Every moment of her life is spent looking for the good, the fun, and the funny aspects of the world we whiz through.

That is why I wrote this book. Most of her antics are funny. Many are painful to imagine really happened. But all of them tell the same important story. No matter what gets put in your way, find a way to make it positive. Find a way to make it enjoyable. If you do that you will be happy. And there is a very good chance people around you will also be a little happier.

An agent asked me a while ago if my book was finished. I said, "How could it be finished? She's still alive. The phone doesn't stop ringing."

My mother called the other night.

"'You are what you drive, so why not be hot?' That's what the ad says, Cam. You should see the picture. It is beautiful. A Camaro. Now, don't tell Kim about this. She will have a stroke. But I can count on you. I need a car. I am so sick of depending on her to drive me around. It's only $23,000. You should see it. You know about buying cars. What do you think my payment would be if I put a little money down on it? It's a V-8! 'You are what you drive, so why not be hot?' I want to be hot. It could be a belated birthday present to myself."

The birthday she had just celebrated was her 90th.

A little bit more before we begin the journey.

My mother married my father shortly after the war. They had a baby girl, Kimberly. My father raised the two boys from my mother's first marriage so much as his own, that one day when I was very young, and Kim and I were riding in the beige Pontiac, she, feeling a bit snarly, turned to me and hissed, "Truman is only your half brother." I pictured him with only half a body. I was very confused.

My father coached my older brothers in little league, adored little "Kimmie," and the family peddled along as families did in the fifties. I came along, eight years after my sister, and after much arguing over a name, I was brought home and brightened things up for a few years.

One constant through all of my mother's years is her zaniness. If she gets an idea in her head, you best just get out of her way. A few years before I was born, my mother and father were sitting before dinner, enjoying a cocktail, and my father mentioned he wished they had a den, but couldn't afford one. My mother said, "Well, then I'll build one."

She did. The next door neighbors were having their house built at that time, so my mother went to the lumber yard and asked for help in ordering supplies, and then each morning copied what the men were doing next door. The only things she didn't do were pour the cement, and install the wiring. But after the cement mixer guy poured the wet cement into the frame she built, she had to ask, "Now what?"

"Well, lady, you need to level it. And fast. You'll need a long two-by-four and another person to hold the other end." One of the workers next door mentioned that it was pretty important to put those big metal bolts she had laying on the ground into the cement while it was still wet. She did both those chores successfully, along with the rest of the job, and, in a reasonable amount of time, she finished.

She was interviewed on the radio when it was done, something that scared her way more than staring at cement drying before she was ready for it to be dry.

Successfully building that room is her favorite memory today, but with one caveat. She was close to the other housewives in the neighborhood before that. But afterwards, the other husbands kept coming home and asking their wives, "So what have you been doing all day while Mrs. Castle is building a room on her house?" Some of the relationships began to sour. My mother, for all the free advice she was getting from the workers next door, would sometimes bring them coffee. It wasn't long before she got wind of the rumor going around the neighborhood that she was giving those workers a lot more than coffee.

My parents had glaring personality differences. My mother wanted a swashbuckler. Unless it was evening, then she wanted to take a bath and read a book. My father was sensitive, gentle and thoughtful. He wanted to be a cartoonist. He was very gregarious, loved to go to parties, loved his cocktails, and possibly around the time my mom wanted to be in the tub, wanted to be a swashbuckler.

It just didn't work.

So, when I was in third grade, they got a divorce.

Before my parents divorced, my time with my dad was limited. He worked so hard at a job he hated, stayed late unwinding at his favorite bar, and spent the weekends trying to not get yelled at by my mother. After the divorce, I got to spend at least one tiptop, quality day each week with my father. He would take me to the zoo, James Bond movies, Cubs games, Bears games, Blackhawk hockey games. He owned the Chicago Flag and Decorating Company, and his best customer was Wrigley Field, where, back then, the Bears also played. Good tickets were a snap.

Also, after the divorce, with the pressure of trying to be happy together removed, my parents discovered that they liked each other. Complete polar opposites in every way, but both possessing fabulous qualities they were then able to admire. My mother's favorite movie was Wuthering Heights. My father's? The Mouse That Roared. To this day my mother cringes at just the title of that movie, she hated it so much.

I can picture, so clearly, being nine or ten years old, and walking into the living room, dressed and ready for my Saturday outing, and having to wait as my mother and father drank coffee and laughed. It was spooky and comforting at the same time.

Years later, after they both remarried, the two couples talked of going on a trip together. Health issues (giant understatement) got in the way of that. But just the fact that it was considered seemed marvelous to me. My father and his second wife, Mackie, who had recently suffered a stroke, moved into the same condo where my mother lived. Mom's third husband, Rudy, had died from a short and vicious bout with cancer. I remember swimming at the condo and coming up from diving deep into the pool. As the water drained off my head, my eyes cleared, and before my ears were able to hear, I focused on my mother and father sitting, facing each other on lawn chairs. They were holding cups of coffee and chortling. I went back under. I came up again and shook my head. It was 30 years after their divorce, and there they were, living four rhododendrons away from each other, and laughing.

My mother and my father taught me that whatever gets hurled at you, if you keep a positive attitude, and try to find a way to make it funny, you will be okay. You might even be better.

So there it is. Follow me on this journey of being raised by a real life version of Lucille Ball in "I Love Lucy."

My mother is crazier than your mother.

Let me show you.

## "Cammie, I Am Going to Take You to See the President."

I was four years old and our President was John Kennedy. My mother heard on the radio that Kennedy was flying into O'Hare airport. She scooped me up and dressed me in Bermuda shorts and a button up short-sleeve shirt. She laced up my brown and white saddle shoes and plopped me in the back seat of our 1960 beige Pontiac. She got behind the wheel and raced out of the north suburbs of Chicago toward O'Hare. I was in my usual position of standing on the back seat and leaning my forearms on the back of the front seat so I could be close to Mom and still see out the front window. Mom had me standing in the back for safety.

When we got close to O'Hare, we were stopped at a roadblock. A police officer walked up to our car and leaned his head in Mom's window. "Where ya headed, Ma'am?"

"I'm taking my son to see the President."

My mother is, for the most part, charming. She can be a spontaneous raging maniac at times, of course, but her basic starting point demeanor is charming. If she needs though, for any reason, to be exceptionally charming it is magical. She blooms into a soft, gentle, enrapturing persona that sometimes, I would think, for a moment, has conjured up soothing background music.

The officer looked at my mother and started to soften. He looked at me. I smiled. He said, "I'll be right back."

He went to his car, chatted a few words to another officer, and then came back. "I am sure not supposed to do this, but . . . what the hey. The President's not landing here. He's landing at the naval base. I'll tell you how to get there." He rattled off some quick directions, that very much unlike today, she understood. He finished with, "Pull off on that gravel road and wait. 'Cause if you hurry you might see him." The officer looked at me again. I saluted him. He slapped the window opening with both hands and said, "Good luck."

My mom pulled a u-turn and raced off. She followed his directions as best as she could remember, and we found ourselves on a gravel road east of O'Hare surrounded by fields closed in with metal fencing. We were the only car on the road. My mom opened her door and got out. She pulled her seat forward, and I crawled out of the back. She picked me up and held me on her hip. It was quiet. There weren't any other cars.

"I hope I followed his directions right. This seems kinda crazy." At that moment we heard a car coming, crunching on the gravel.  "It's him! It's him!" My mom yelled. "Look, it's a limo! A big black limo!"

A large black limo pulled past us. There was a driver, and in the back window was President Kennedy. He gave us a big smile as the car crunched past us, no more than three feet away. We waved like crazy. "He's even more handsome in person. He's so tan. Did you see how white his teeth are? Cammie, you got to see the President! Oh, my." She set me down and let out a big sigh. "My goodness. That was awfully nice of that officer, wouldn't you say? Well, let's go home."

\* \* \*

One day when my son, Carter, was an infant, I heard on the radio that President G.W. Bush was coming to Seattle. I scooped up my son and placed him in his multi-strapped, molded, reinforced, polypropylene car seat and said, "Let's go to the beach."

## My Mother Moved Three Times without Telling Me

**M**y mother moved three times without telling me. Yup. This is not a sad story. Just listen.

I was in the third grade. There were Mom and Dad, and my sister Kim, sixteen, living at home. My two older brothers, Truman, twenty-one, and Steve, nineteen, were off at college. I was playing with my army men on the living room rug when my mother called, "Kim. Cam. Dinners ready. Oh, sit down. I have something to tell you. Ah, what is it? Ah . . . yeah. Your father and I got a divorce, and I bought a new house! We'll go look at it after dinner. Well, dinners getting cold so let's go eat."

After dinner we got in the car and drove three houses down and two to the left. It was pouring rain. We peeked into the windows of our new house, got back in the car, and left.

On the last day of school of the third grade, about three months later, I was walking home, "No more pencils, no more books, no more teachers . . . huh?"

Our house was empty. There was no furniture, only Mary, our very large and very wonderful cleaning lady, vacuuming.

Mary said to me, "What? You know where the new house is, don't you? Grab a lawn chair and walk on down there."

So I did.

I looked into the picture window of our new house. All I saw was furniture, just pressed up against the window. All that furniture and stuff from our old big house just crammed into this little, white house.

When I turned left and walked past those two houses, I crossed over the line into a new school district. Instead of walking to school, pretending to be James Bond, and shooting bad guys, and finding new secret paths, and saving beautiful young women on the way . . .

I had to ride the bus.

I was now the farthest kid from the school, so I was the first one picked up and the last one dropped off. The bus driver's name was Emo. Weirdest looking guy I had ever seen. Turned out to be a cool guy. He would park his bus in front of our house in the morning and wait for me to come out. I felt pretty special. I didn't actually like my old school and ended up loving the new one.

The new house was pretty cool also. It was heated with oil heat, in the floor. So in the winter, when you got out of bed, you stepped on a toasty warm floor. The back yard was enclosed with multiple colors of lilac trees. I loved that home, and we lived there for years.

My sister went away to college. Now it was just my mom and me. We had a good relationship. She trusted me and gave me a lot of freedom.

I had a ton of friends. The high school I went to had 3600 kids. I was friends with different groups: the hippies, the swimmers, the theatre people. My junior year was fabulous. I finally even had a girl friend I was crazy about. Things couldn't get any better.

I was coming home on the last day of school before summer vacation.

"No more pencils, no more books, no more teacher's dirty . . . what?"

There was a moving van in front of our house. My mother was standing beside the open back of this huge truck.

I said, "Mom? What's . . . ?"

"Oh, we're moving to Seattle to be with your brother and sister. We don't have to go today. Just the furniture needs to go today."

At that moment the movers carried my bed past me and put it on the truck.

A few years earlier, my brother, Truman and his wife had moved from Toledo, Ohio, to Seattle after some friends of his showed them some slides of a visit to the Pacific Northwest. Simple.

When my sister got married, her new husband said, "We can live anywhere. Where would you like that to be?"

"Seattle," she said. "To be near my brother."

So, after giving it way less thought, my mother decided to move the two of us there also.

We didn't go that day. I was so mad I went off and stayed at different friends' houses for three days and made her wait for me in our charming and now empty beautiful cozy house on Arbor Lane in Glenview, Illinois. All that my mom had left in that house to pass the time until I would return and agree to be dragged to Seattle was her book, one pillow, and a lamp.

When I resurfaced, my mother, in an effort to show her true thoughtfulness for my feelings, or possibly an attempt to ease her mind over the very real possibility that during the drive I might kill her, offered to let my girlfriend, Hannah, come on the trip with us.

It was a smart move.

The three of us drove across the country to Seattle.

We stayed at Truman's house. Hannah soon flew back to Chicago. Previously unknown to me, Truman was moving to a new house, so we purchased his. We moved into this wonderful house in an area called Cherry Crest, so named because of all of the cherry trees that blossomed in the spring. We had a view of Mount Rainier, Lake Washington and the Space Needle. Across the street was a guy just my age. Jerry. A great guy, and years later, the best man in my wedding (not to Hannah, by the way). There were girls our age on either side of our houses. The house had a big front yard where Jerry and I ran long football pass patterns. We planted a garden. The asparagus Truman had previously planted was coming up all over the place. (By the way, the scientific time it takes asparagus to grow to the point of being harvested is this; exactly one year after the person who has planted it has moved away. It is true. Just ask anybody. Except anybody who has planted it because they wouldn't know because they have been gone at least a year.) I loved that house.

The next fall, I went off to college in Bellingham, Washington. My mother and my sister drove me up to the campus and just dropped me off. I was standing there in front of the dorms. And they just drove off. See ya. So I dragged my trunk up to an older, helpful looking student and asked, "Where's Beeta?"

"You mean Beta?" he snarled, and then pointed me off in the wrong direction.

When I finally found my dorm room, I opened the door and startled my roommate to be. He turned and glared at me over his shoulder. He looked to me like a Mongol warrior. He was a big guy with thick black hair that was all askew. He tilted his head and looked at me with squinty eyes. He was terrifying. "Hi, I'm Mike. Wanna smoke a joint?"

Mike, I very soon found out, was the most pleasant, polite, thoughtful, and talented person (first chair concert bassoon player) anybody has ever had the chance to have as a roommate. We got along famously and had loads of fun.

One day we were lying on our beds, and the phone rang. Mike got up to get it.

"Cam. It's your mom." He handed me the phone with the very long cord.

My mother said to me, "I've sold the house and bought a condo. The house was just . . ."

I said, "Fuck you." And threw the handset across the room.

It was just spinning on the tile floor. Mike said, with very wide eyes, "Would you like me to hang that up?"

The condo was fantastic. It had a cabana with a Jacuzzi and a ping-pong table. It had a swimming pool with a diving board. I loved it. My friends and I had hours of fun at that condo.

So, if I ever wonder about if I should feel bad about my mother moving three times without telling me, I just think about how each time it seemed like my life turned for the better. And if that doesn't work, I just remember standing by that hot tub and saying to the very nice girl, "Do you want to take a Jacuzzi?"

And she said, "I don't have a suit."

# Piccalilli, Polio and Poots

"**C**ammie! What are you doing? Put down that hose. Were you drinking out of that? I have told you a hundred times, 'If you drink out of a garden hose you will get strep throat.' How many times do I have to say it? Put it down. Don't look at me like that. It's true. Come here."

My mother knelt down and put her hands on my little shoulders.

"If you drink out of a garden hose, you *will* get strep throat. Just don't do it again. Why don't you run on inside."

"Oh," she shouted. ". . . and take off that wet suit. If you keep a wet suit on you will get POLIO!"

I now occasionally drink right from a garden hose, but not without ever so briefly considering the possible ramifications. I do find myself quite squirmy if I am still wearing a wet bathing suit well after the time I might return to the water.

What our parents say to us, pound into our little heads, stays with us throughout the rest of our lives. Everyone lives with that fact. It's no big deal. Only my mother's warnings were incessant. The rules and warnings came from all over the place. Old wives' tales told as absolute fact were flying around my little head like racquetballs ricocheting off the walls of the court in a mismatch.

"If you sleep with air blowing on you, you will be paralyzed!"

To this day I cannot sleep in a room with any moving air. If the person next to me on an airplane points his air-schnozzle thing at me, I fall into a panic attack. I not only become unreasonably cold, but in the dark recesses of my subconscious, I fear that if I were to drift asleep with this stream of air blowing directly on me, and I *were* to awake, I would awake most certainly without the use of my arms and legs.

My mother told me I should always leave one bite of food on my plate. That way, she reasoned, the hostess knows she has served you just the right amount of food. If you leave more than that, you have been served too much, or it wasn't properly prepared. If you clean your plate, it sends a message that you might not have been served enough. This tidbit of wisdom has stuck with me so tightly that I will sometimes have one bite left on my plate when I am alone and still hungry. I look at that bite, sitting there, and marvel at the power harmless phrases uttered during our formative years have on us. I recognize how ridiculous that is, then I carry my plate to the sink and wash that one bite down the drain.

Luckily not all of my mother's unique theories stuck. Some must have been tossed at me after my formative years, where one's psyche turns from a sponge to something like Flubber.

For example, we recently went on a long road trip with my fifteen-year-old son, Max. He was wonderful, but my advice for him is absorbed as if mopping up a spill with aluminum foil.

Advice like, "Don't walk so close to that cliff." is deflected with a response like, "Yeah, whatever. I'm fine. Don't worry about it."

Or, if the advice is really important, more important than, let's say, not falling off a cliff, and it is offered with some sense of urgency, it is usually reflected with the simple, "Chill, Dad."

So, luckily, some of my mother's wisdom just bounced off.

She used to say, "I never wear my seat belt. You know why? Because I saw on the news that a woman was in a horrible crash, and she would have surely been killed, but she wasn't wearing her seat belt. So, she was thrown from the car and landed on some soft grass. I am not about to be strapped into this big piece of metal when we go crashing into something. I want to been thrown to safety."

One day she had me help her drag all her plants out of her bedroom.

"Why are we doing this, Mom?"

"I constantly have headaches, and I figured out why. These damn plants have been sucking the oxygen out of my room."

"But . . . Mom . . . aw, forget it."

Then there is the language: family pet names or phrases for things ranging from food or household items, to bodily functions. Growing up, I didn't know that my mother's vocabulary was unique unto our household.

"Fordcast." You know, the part of the Sunday paper that you use to look up what's on TV. The words, "TV Guide," were never uttered in our house. It was, "Bring me the fordcast!" A friend would be over. "Scott, can you hand me the fordcast? I want to see who Johnny has on tonight."

"The what?" my friend would ask.

I just recently asked my mother how she spelled "fordcast."

"F-O-R-E-C-A-S-T. You know."

"No, Mom, it was F-O-R-D-C-A-S-T."

"That is ridiculous. Fordcast doesn't mean anything. It's the forecast. Everybody knows that. It tells you what's on TV."

So I called my two brothers and my sister. "When we were kids and we wanted to see what was on TV, where did we look?"

"In the fordcast." they all replied.

Picklelily. We always had a jar of picklelily in the fridge. Trouble is, no one else I ever met outside our immediate family ever heard of picklelily. Sweet relish, like the kind you put on a hot dog, was picklelily.

I called my mom and asked her how she spelled picklelily.

"I don't know, just look on the jar. Every refrigerator in America has a jar of picklelily in it. Just open up the door and read the label."

So I googled picklelily. And after a bit of poking around I found it.

"Piccalilli. A relish made from green tomatoes and vinegar, originating in old England."

For fun, next time you see someone, ask him or her if they have heard of piccalilli. If they say yes, and they can tell you what it is, go buy a lottery ticket.

LBT. "What do you feel like for lunch, Cammie? How about an LBT?"

Many times in a restaurant I would ask, "Do you have an LBT?" And the answer was always a blank stare, or "No."

I would say, "You know, lettuce, bacon, tomato . . . on toast. You must have that."

"You mean a BLT?"

"What's that?" I would ask.

Now, it's not that our mother has a poor vocabulary. She is well read and speaks very well.

Unless she has to say Massachusetts, Switzerland, or God forbid, quesadilla. Those three she has a problem with for some reason, the latter being such an ordeal for her that we mischievously encourage her to say it as often as possible. It never comes out the same two times in a row, and for some reason, her version doesn't contain four syllables, but usually six or seven.

"Hey Mom, this looks good." one of us would say, pointing at the menu. "You've had it before and liked it. Why don't you order it?"

"Okay," she says, falling for the trap. Looking up at the waiter, she orders with the deliberate confidence of the spelling bee winner, pronouncing the word they have just correctly spelled.

"I will have the . . . koo-ace a-dilly-ah."

None though, have had the effect of two words that were pervasive in my childhood. Two words that were, unbeknownst to me, completely unique to our household.

"Deedee" and "Poots."

Those are the pet names my mother gave for going to the bathroom. I have never met anyone whose family used those two words to describe those activities. I didn't know we were the only folks using those words. Imagine my embarrassment as a seven-year-old asking the camp counselor if I can go deedee. It gets worse. What does the deedee come out of? The deedee's home, of course! I shudder at the thought that I must have said to someone, sometime, "I have to go poots."

"Doctor, my poots' home hurts." Ugh. That is just not fair to a child. Call it what you want at home, but warn your little ones that if they refer to those words in the outside world, people will think they are nuts.

I had no idea where the words came from. I cannot even stand talking about it. I feared they were a form of onomatopoeia. I would have preferred to call it onomatopoeia.

"Wait up for me. I'll be right there. I just have to go onomatopoeia."

When I was eight-years-old, I still thought deedee and poots were common terms. I used them freely. At that age, most of your conversations, mostly ones about bathroom stuff, you carry on with your family. No problem.

That was the year we moved to the new house. I remember one fateful day. I was playing in the front yard when three kids came bounding down the street. In the lead was a pretty girl with long, blond, wavy hair.

Two little kids, a boy and a girl, were running behind her, trying to keep up.

The girl came right up to me and said, "Hi. I'm Wendy. I live down the street. Did you just move in? You seem nice. Do you want to play? Oh, and here are my brother and sister. They're younger. Say hi," she said to them. "Their names are Deedee and Poots. Well, those aren't their real names, those are nicknames. But that's what we call them. What's your name?"

I thought my head was going to explode. How is this possible? Seeing as, in my mind, at that time, I thought everybody *went* deedee and poots! It's like meeting someone's kids, and hearing, "Hi, I would like you to meet my children, Piss and Crap." My mind was reeling. How could this be? Turns out, of course, that family never conceived someone would use their cute little children's nicknames to refer to going to the bathroom.

The other day I asked my mother where "deedee and poots" came from. She said that her mother called it "doing your duty." Not doody, but duty, like an order or an obligation. Plus, her mother said it very sternly. My mother and her younger brother just hated that, so they decided to make up their own words, just for themselves. My mother's younger brother decided to call going to the bathroom "picking violets."

My mother just made up "deedee and poots." I guess in retrospect it could have been worse. At least I didn't walk up to the rifle range instructor at military camp, when I was twelve, and ask, "Sir, may I be excused? I need to pick some violets."

So, today, when my kids are lounging around in wet bathing suits, I don't say a word. I find myself biting my bottom lip, but I don't say a word. They look in the TV Guide to see when "South Park" is on. And if nature calls, they go to the bathroom. That's it.

Well, it's time for lunch, so I am going to go downstairs and make everybody an LBT.

# My Mother and Our Pets

**M**y mother loved pets, just not for very long. We always referred to her as the assassin. Two things about that title are: one, that moniker is not really accurate, and two, she didn't mind it. Throughout our childhoods, my two brothers, my sister and I were given many pets. And they all met an unusual demise. I will list some of them here, but the complete list is far too vast and still partially unknown. It's all right, if, while reading this, you laugh, we all have. For us, I think it's just a form of therapy. For you, it would be only morbid pleasure. But what the heck, here we go.

## PINK NOSE

My older brother Steve had a cat, Pink Nose. He loved that cat and had it for awhile. Pink Nose was a good cat and had only one bad habit: having diarrhea on the chenille bedspreads that were on my brother's twin beds. Really, he mostly had diarrhea on my other brother, Truman's bed. My mother was sure that Pink Nose could sense the sibling rivalry between my brothers, and in a show of loyalty, would desecrate Truman's bed. Who knows? Our mother really loved those bedspreads. They were beige, and though colored coordinated with Pink Nose's morning contribution, the daily ritual of dealing with the mess and stench took its toll on her.

So, one afternoon when my brothers were not home, something Pink Nose ate that definitely did not agree with him, ended up on the beloved, beige, chenille bedspread. Pink Nose ended up in the car, going for a ride. A familiar scene, like one from the movie, "The Godfather Meets Doctor Doolittle," Pink Nose was going for "the ride." You see, when our mother finally had it with one of our pets, she would take them for a ride far out into the countryside and drop them off in some beautiful surroundings. Then she'd rationalize, "This animal would be so much happier on a farm, running free, a healthier life, fresh air, mice to catch. Oh, Pink Nose, you will be so happy. GET IN THE CAR."

"Where's Pink Nose?" asked Steve.

"I don't know," answered our mother.

In the crime of pet disposal, the answer of "I don't know" is really all that's needed. "Must have run away. I'm so sorry."

My brothers were sad. But time heals. Then one afternoon, my brother Steve heard a scratch at the window.

"PINK NOSE! You're back!"

There he was, scrawny, dirty, tired, but he came back. He jumped through the open window into Steve's arms. Steve was so happy. A miracle. What had Pink Nose eaten along the way to survive? Don't know. But I do know that it ended up on the chenille bedspread.

# STEVE'S TROPICAL FISH

My brother Steve bred Guppies. Prize Guppies. He had many fish tanks gurgling all over their bedroom. One evening while he was out on a wintry night in Chicago, the power went out. The heaters in the tanks weren't working. Our mother was very concerned. She did care, especially because it was a crisis that she needed to jump into.

"Oh, my, Steve's prize fish are going to freeze. I have to do something. Oh, look at that. The male is holding the pregnant female up. It must be warmer at the top. This is horrible. What can I do?"

She put them on the gas stove.

Over the pilot light.

Forgot about them.

Steve came home. Walked through the kitchen.

"Hmm? What's on the stove? "AHHH!"

# TEXAS SUN LIZARD

Mom took me to the pet store one day. She'd heard once that the only thing they could find that was consistent in the background of convicted murderers was that none of them had pets when they were kids. So she bought us pets. But then she would get sick of them. A pet couldn't have any bad habits if it were to last in the household. But our mother's scope of bad habits was rather large, and a tad unforgiving. If the animal, let's say, went to the bathroom, it was likely scoring some negative points. Needing to be fed "all the time" didn't help their cause much either. (I wonder if someday there will be a study of convicts that did have pets, yet their mothers did them all in.)

We picked out a lizard. A Texas Sun Lizard! He was really cool. My mom sprung for all the accessories: the tank, the gravel, the log, the special little water bowl, the special food. We took him home. It was a beautiful sunny day in Glenview, Illinois. Hmm. Sunny day. Texas Sun Lizard. Let's put him outside. Good idea. So we did.

When I went back out later to check on him, he was . . . stiff. Lying on his back on the log. Stiff. His legs were sticking straight out. "Mom?!"

We went back to the pet store. My mother stood in front of the pet store guy, holding my lizard by the tail, which was pointing up like a Texas Sun Lizard satay.

"What the hell is wrong with this lizard? We took him home and put him out in the sun, and look at this. What kind of a pet store is this?"

"You put him out in the sun?"

"Of course we did. He's a sun lizard isn't he?"

"That's just a name. He's nocturnal. You can't put him in the sun. What were you thinking?"

"What? If he can't be in the sun than why in the hell don't you call him a Texas Moon Lizard?!"

## MY TURTLES

I had two cute little turtles in that small clear donut shaped turtle trough that was so popular until they found out that these particular turtles were carrying salmonella. So you can't buy them anymore. Even though I never heard of any of my classmates (75% of whom had these little supposedly infested companions) coming down with salmonella. I can only guess that would mean that one would suddenly be overtaken with the desire to swim upstream. Anyway, I had these turtles and I liked them very much. One interesting thing they used to do was try to escape. Their plan went like this. One would climb on the other's back and crawl over the wall and be out. Then I would find him and put him back in. I was sure it was always the same one that got out.

"Give me a boost. I'll come back for you." And the other one always fell for it.

So, one day I came home and went into my room and checked on my turtles. "Hmm. They're both gone. That's odd."

"Mom?"

She was in her bed reading a book. "Yes?"

"My turtles are both gone. Do you . . . ?"

"Oh, my God." She jumped out of bed, and headed for the patio door. "I'm so sorry. They looked so sickly. I felt they needed some fresh air. I put them out for a walk. Just a short one. I thought it would be good for them."

"How long ago?"

"What time is it?"

"Four o'clock."

"Ah . . . ah, three hours ago."

## OUR PARAKEET

We had this bird for longer than I had been alive. I was little, and this bird was always in the dining room in his cage. He was a good bird. Blue. Stoic. I loved that bird.

One day my mother noticed that we had an ant problem. There were ants making a trail from the kitchen to the dining room. They were congregating under the birdcage. Hmm. So she got the Raid and let those ants have it. Killed them all right under the birdcage. Our parakeet stiffened up and expired. Still clutching the little wooden bar he perched and swung on. Still holding the bar. Only now he was upside down and stiff. I loved that bird. Guess who found him?

"Mom?!"

"Oops."

## MY SISTER''S CAT ANGEL

My sister's boyfriend went off to Vietnam. She was so distraught that our mother got her a cat. Angel. That was her boyfriend's last name. Angel was a short hair, gray and white, lovely and intelligent cat. Angel, I think, set the record for longevity within our mother's care. My sister Kim went off to college, and it was only Mom and me and Angel. Angel always came when you called her. That was the good news. The bad news was to get her attention, we had to call her name in an ascending high-pitched squeal that had to decrease to a drowned out "LLL" Like this: "aaaaaaaanngg…eeeeelllll!" It worked. But it was humiliating if someone, like the cute neighbor girl, heard you, a 17-year-old boy, squeal it. Angel moved with us from Chicago to Seattle. She was holding her own. That was until she developed this annoying habit of going down to the end of the hall, turning around next to my mother's bedroom door, waiting until she made eye contact with my mother, raising up her hind quarters, jutting her tail up into the air and . . . spraying some horrible fluid directly on the wall so it could seep down into the blue shag carpeting. I am sure that she only did it when she had my mother's attention. Why? This was a smart cat. Had my mother done something to her? Not yet. I do not know why Angel did that. But all I know is that if you take that horribly irritating squeal to get Angel to come home, and multiply it by 10, that still does not equal the sound that came out of my sweet mother's mouth as she watched Angel spray paint the hall wall.

Well, Angel lasted until I went to college. I left. It was just Mom and the cat. It made me feel better knowing that, though I was the last child to leave, Mom still had a little companion. Yeah, sure. On my second visit back . . .

"Where's Angel?"

"I don't know. She must have missed you so much. I bet she's on her way up to find you. You know those cats. So resourceful. Remember Pink Nose? Or was that before your time?"

"Mom, Pink Nose walked home. Not away from home. Their homing device brings them *home,* not to some dorm room in college following the scent of a trunk!"

But she convinced me once again of her innocence. And what the heck, I don't know that Angel was taken on "the ride."

## MY WHITE MICE

My mother bought me two white mice. We brought them home, put the cedar chips in the cage, fed them some pellets, got the little water siphon to work and went to bed. What we didn't do was latch the door. So in the morning there were no mice in the cage.

"Mom?!"

They were gone. I found one in the living room. Ew. Well, I found some of one in the living room and none of the other. You see, I had a dog, Pepi. A poodle. A wonderful dog that shows up in this story later. So Pepi got the mice. That's not his fault. I think it's really his job, contrary to some popular belief that a poodle's job is to wear ridiculous hairstyles or outfits and dance and play the piano. (I saw my aunt's poodle play the piano, and it was very interesting, and the dog seemed to love it.) Besides having a stupid name, a poodle can be a very good dog. But anyway, Pepi ate my mice. And I was very upset. So my mother, always kind and wanting to keep me out of the penitentiary, bought me two more mice. This time we latched the door. The mice survived the night and did quite well for quite a while. One summer day while I was off at camp, my mother decided to clean my room.

"What a mess. And oh, what a stink. I'll clean out this mouse cage. I think I should put them outside. Fresh air. It will be good for them. I'll just set them here. On the rotisserie." (A copper topped rotisserie.)

I came home from camp. "Whoa. What a clean room. Huh? Where are my mice? Mom?!"

"Yes?"

"Mom. Where are my mice?"

"Oh, they're outside, on the patio. Getting some fresh air."

"Okay, thanks." I went outside and there was my mouse cage on top of the copper rotisserie. In summer. In Chicago. There was one mouse in the cage. Cooked. The other somehow had squeezed his way out. Pepi got him in the front yard.

About a month later, Truman was visiting. He and our mom were talking, and I was in the kitchen getting a pop, when I saw something out of the corner of my eye. A mouse. A white mouse! It ran behind the washing machine in the pantry. The one unaccounted for mouse. The one I always secretly held out hope that it-had-somehow-survived mouse!

"Truman. Mom. My mouse. My mouse. It's back! Come quick. Come quick!"

"Yeah, yeah. Sure. Whatever. So anyways, Truman tell me about..."

"Come quick. Come quick. It's my mouse."

I finally convinced them to reluctantly humor me and pretend to look for the mouse. My brother put some peanut butter on a spoon and crouched next to the washer, looking at my mother like "aren't I the best brother in the world?" when a white mouse ran out from under the washer and dashed by the spoon.

Truman shouted, "Get the cage! Get the cage!"

We caught the mouse, and I was very happy. I could not believe one of the first two mice survived.

"Uh, oh. What's this? He has a goiter!"

My beloved, reborn, Pepi surviving, macho, super mouse, that I had named Rambo, had a goiter under his tail. It was huge. Darn. He had come so far. What should we do?

A few days later I looked into Rambo's cage. "Huh? What the heck is this?"

There were thirteen gray baby mice.

"Rambo? What have you done?"

While he was in the garage all those weeks, he was obviously violated by a wild gray mouse. And now he was a mother! We now had Rambolina and thirteen little pencil erasers in the cage. The problem was that these mixed race mice were a little high strung. If you were to, let's say, drop the lid on the cage after setting down the food dish, and it went clank, the thirteen little, pink babies would suddenly go berserk. They would start jumping about, and they were smaller than the spaces between the wires of the cage. They would bounce out of the cage all over the place. So the game was to grab a shoebox and start tossing them into it while they jumped out of it like some feeble physics class demonstration of how a nuclear reaction works. They were bouncing out almost as fast as we could put them in. Eventually they would calm down and be all back in the cage.

I went off on a two-week vacation and asked my mom to take care of my new mice village. Looking back, what was I thinking? When I got back, there was Rambolina and one baby mouse in a bowl with Saran Wrap with holes punched in it in the garage.

"Mom?!"

"What? The cage stunk. I saved one baby for you. How many did you need? The mom or dad or whatever it is, is fine. I took the others to Harms Woods. (Harms Woods was a forest preserve right near our neighborhood that was a depository for many of our pets that were, let's say, considered, short distance non-returners.)

So, the twelve baby mice of mixed background were introduced into Harms Woods, where, if they survived, they met up with some other temporary animal guests of the Castle household.

# MY DOG PEPI

I got him when I was about eight. Pepi was a toy poodle. That designation being another societal slur on this poor breed of dog. Toy? He was a cool dog. He wasn't a "toy." He was a stud. Really. We always let his hair grow. He always came when we called. He loved to ride in the car. I loved that dog. And he never did anything wrong. Ah . . . well, he did eat anything plastic, like my army men. And he did every once in a while do this strange maneuver of sitting on the floor, raising his back legs up, and dragging by his front feet, his icky butt across the white living room carpet. Mom really hated that. Pepi had nine lives. Well, really it turned out to be only five.

He was hit by a bus. A city bus. And on the bus was the nice man, a carpenter who had just redone our cabinets. He recognized Pepi, got off the bus, picked him up and had the bus driver take the bus down the street to our house. I can still see all the faces of the people on this city bus, way off the route, watching this carpenter deliver the wounded dog to its home. We took him to the vet, and Pepi was okay. His hip was kind of screwed up, but it healed, and he was okay.

Until he was shot.

The lady that lived behind us hated Pepi. He supposedly would poop in her flowerbeds. He might have occasionally. Or always. But he's a dog. And I think he hated her, too. One night my mom was out getting ready to call Pepi in when she saw the wicked old neighbor lady crouched near the flowerbeds calling Pepi's name, with what looked like a revolver in her hand. My mother quickly called Pepi in. Hmm. So when Pepi came in one night with a 22-caliber bullet hole in his thigh, we had a feeling who did it. Mom! No. The neighbor lady. But there was no way to prove it, since the incriminating circumstantial evidence came from our mother. So, we let it go. The vet fixed him up. And he was okay.

Until he was stabbed.

We never knew what the stab wound was from. It was very odd. It was a curly Q in shape, in the middle of his back. Our only farfetched guess was that it was from a spring in the couch that he always laid under. It was ugly and looked very painful. But it healed and he was okay.

That was until . . .

He could romp in the snow in zero degree weather and chase tennis balls in ninety-degree heat. He roamed freely in the neighborhood. He survived everything. Almost everything.

My mom gave him away.

She gave him away. She pulled that "I don't know" routine with me. But it didn't fly. I freaked out. And you know what? She caved in. She confessed. We went to these strangers' house, and she asked, and she got my dog back. Pepi was back. Dragging his poopy butt along the carpet like before, and all was right with the world.

A year or so later Pepi was missing.

"Mom? Where's Pepi?"

"Gee, I don't know. He was old. He must have finally run away."

After all he had been through, I realized he was gone. Really gone. Poor Pepi. I eventually got over it. I missed him, but I was in high school and very busy. Life went on. Then one day I was in the car with my brother Steve driving. Next to him was his wife Linda. I was beside her. She is about the sweetest and most well meaning person on the planet. She, before this particular ride, had uncharacteristically, downed a couple of glasses of wine. For some reason the topic of dogs came up, and I, feeling melancholy, brought up Pepi. "I sure miss him."

Linda started to sniff like she was about to sneeze.

I said, "I loved that dog. I wish he hadn't run away."

She started to bob up and down and make quiet snorting sounds.

"What? Why are you doing that? Is there something I don't know?"

Linda burst out one large laugh then stopped herself and said, "Steve! I'm so sorry. I thought he knew."

"Linda!"

"What? What? Knew what?"

"Oh, Linda you might as well tell him."

So she did. Turns out Pepi didn't run away. Mom took him to the vet. After the vet checked him out, he said that Pepi was an old dog, and probably only had one year left. As my mother was paying the bill, there was a man with his young son standing next to my mom and Pepi.

"What a nice dog," said the man.

"Why, thank you."

"I want to get my son a dog, but we have to move away in a year, so we can't really get a dog."

"Really?" my mom said. "Well, this one's only good for a year. Do you want this one?"

She gave him my dog.

Pepi!

If it weren't for a few glasses of Asti Spumanti and Linda's low tolerance for alcohol, I would have never known. I wish I didn't.

Well, our mom was not good with pets. But she has always tried to be good with people. She made that stranger and that boy happy and figured she was saving me from seeing my beloved dog in his waning days. She was so good about the buying the pet part. It was just the keeping them part she was never very good at. There isn't ever a vicious thought in her, but merely a desire to make things better for everyone. Pooping in the fresh fields of a lovely farm in central Illinois as opposed to pooping on the heirloom bedspreads is better for everybody. Our mother has always meant well. All that is important to remember is that, no matter who you are, as long as you don't "go" on anything made of fabric, you will not have to worry about going for "the ride."

# The Operation was a Success but the Patient Died

To be completely fair and transparent, my mother actually saved as many pets as she did in. The number of those on the plus side, though, all came during one event. That event being a C-section she performed on one of Steve's prize guppies.

One evening Steve came rushing into the room where Mom was reading a book.

"She's dead. She's dead!"

"Who, for Pete's sake?"

"My momma guppy. She'd been with me the longest. A prize. She had so many babies. She's dead, and she was just about to give birth. I know it."

I will pause here to fill in any not tuned into the gestation habits of guppies. They are live breeders. They don't lay eggs and tirelessly dote over them. Nope. The momma guppy gets fat as hell, then one day, out of two dark spots on her side, baby guppies pop out. Tons of them. Up to one hundred sometimes. They dart around. They are very quick. And that is because the momma, in a manner that would be frowned upon in human circles, eats them. As fast as she can. Plan being, I am sure, that the strongest and quickest survive.

"I know what to do, Steve. A Cesarean section. I can do it. Hell, I have had four of them. Bring her to me in the bathroom."

So Steve carried the expired and plump mother to the bathroom. Our mother laid the fish on some tissue paper, and with a razor blade, made an incision. (When I asked recently if she gave her a bikini cut, she sneezed a "no" at me.) She took the fish back to the tank and carefully and gently squeezed. Lo and behold, scores of little darting baby guppies swam to freedom. An added feature was the momma wasn't there to eat most of them.

So Steve had a "mother lode" of baby guppies, granted without a refined gene pool, and was momentarily in awe with our mother.

# Baby Teeth

One of my mother's many idiosyncrasies was a tremendous aggressive aversion to a loose tooth in one of her children's mouths. She couldn't stand it. If it was loose, it had to come out.

Most young kids would probably prefer to wait until the baby tooth falls out on its own, rather than pull it out themselves. They fear that quick sting of pain and any ensuing blood. There are many little kids around the world at any given moment with the tip of their tongues holding onto the top of a semi-loose tooth and slightly wriggling it. Wriggling it back and forth, gradually making it loosen. To a little kid, it's really an interesting phenomenon that your tooth falls out in the first place. Add to that, as a little kid, you have the control over when the final dramatic event is going to take place. This is one rare event when a young kid actually has control over something.

That is unless you happened to be birthed by my mother. The mere thought of a loose tooth in a child's mouth would consume her with an intense desire to experience the incredibly satisfying catharsis obtained only by extracting that tooth, regardless of the wishes of the tooth owner.

Early on I learned about my mother's obsession. "Look, Mom, one of my toofs is loose!"

"Oh, really? Let me see."

She gently put her index finger in my mouth, which was open like a hungry baby bird's, and perused around until she found the wiggler. Then, with the speed and dexterity of a magician performing a card trick, she got two fingers on the tooth and ripped it out with a loud "YAH!" That tooth was nowhere near falling out on its own. It hurt and bled. That was bad, but the scream - the "YAH!"- was the worst part. It had a hideous, triumphant tone that still echoes in my and my siblings' heads.

Years later, when talking to my brothers and sister, I learned she yanked out all of their teeth also. Poor Truman and Steve, my mother confessed to me, had to endure the string on the tooth tied to the slamming door knob trick, right out of a Three Stooges episode.

After she yanked out my tooth, I screamed, "Why did you do that?"

She said, "It was loose. It had to come out eventually. I don't want it to come out in the night and have you swallow it."

Yeah? Sure. She just loved pulling them out.

She was very satisfied. That time I think she even remembered to put a quarter under my pillow.

I learned. I never again mentioned that I had a loose tooth. But she was relentless. During baby tooth harvest time, she was like a hawk circling above the field searching for the slightest motion, the slightest sign of prey.

I was watching Bugs Bunny or Foghorn Leghorn, enrapt in the show. Unconsciously my tongue slid over to the loose tooth and wriggled it. I wriggled it back and forth slightly a few times. Then something exciting happened in the cartoon, like the dog rushing out of his doghouse and chasing the big rooster until he abruptly ran out of chain. My tongue wriggled the tooth faster.

Then . . . I never knew when the hawk was circling . . . I was caught. She swooped down on me. My sweet and generous mother seemed, for just a fleeting moment, to transform into the Wicked Witch of The West, hovering in the air in front of me saying, "Do you have a loose tooth, My Pretty? Ha. Ha. Ha. Ha. Ha."

With my irresponsible tongue covering the innocent tooth like hiding the cookie jar behind my back, I said, "Nwo."

Then she transformed back into Mom, and said in a calm voice, "Oh, I think you do. I saw you wiggle it. Here, just let me check."

"Nwo."

"Here, let me just wiggle it. I won't pull it out if it's not ready."

"Nwo."

"Here, I'll just use one finger. I couldn't possibly pull out a tooth with one finger. Look, I'll use my pinkie finger." With her head tilted, her bottom lip slightly out, eyes like a puppy, she held her pinkie finger up in front of my little face. "See. I couldn't pull a tooth out with this. Okay?"

"Mokay."

"Open up. Is this the one?"

"Uh huh."

"YAH!!!" She yanked it out. With her one pinkie finger. I couldn't believe it. It hurt. It bled. It wasn't ready. It was in her hand. And she was so happy.

I never fell for the pinkie trick again.

So, the next time she spied my undisciplined tongue giving away the farm, and she begged "to just check," I refused. I was a little older, a little wiser, and I was the last child she was going to have. The last set of baby teeth. That wiggling tooth was to her like the last dose of heroin an addict might get.

She started to look at me quite strangely.

I went, "Mwom?" My tongue helplessly trying to protect its charge.

"I want that tooth."

"Nwo. Nwo."

She took a step forward.

I took a step back.

She took two steps forward.

I took off running.

She tackled me from behind and reached her hand around my head and into my mouth. She strummed her fingers against my teeth and yanked out my last baby tooth.

Really.

I mean it. Really.

I was lying on the living room floor, and she was kneeling beside me. In her fingers, held like a three-carat diamond, was my tooth.

So, as you can guess, my kids' baby teeth dangled like over-ripe Rainier cherries on a tree limb until *they* were ready to remove them. And when one of my kids would say to me "hey, Dad, I think I have a loose toof," a panicky chill would waft over me.

Then I would say, "It's okay. That thing will probably just fall out on its own."

When it did, I'd put five bucks under their pillow.

# My Mother, a Babysitter, and New Math.

**M**y mother and I were driving in the beige Pontiac. It was early evening on a winter night in Chicago. We were in the north edges of the big city, having driven down from the North Shore town of Glenview.

"I had the hardest time finding a sitter. I can't believe it. It was just crazy. Luckily Mary overheard me while she was sweeping. She said a friend of hers babysits. Way down here in Chicago, but Mary said she is very nice and a good sitter. I'm sure you'll like her. I trust Mary. She's been our cleaning lady for years. She's been Bessie's cleaning lady even longer. I trust her. Hmm. Hand me that slip of paper. This is the address. Hmm. Not the best of neighborhoods is it? Well, get in the back seat. I'll go knock on the door. Oh, here she comes. That's nice. Get in the back, Cam. Go on."

I pulled on the lever and pushed on the heavy passenger side door. Using my shoulder, I managed to creak the door open enough for it to catch and stay open. I stepped out and pulled the passenger half of the big bench seat forward and crawled behind it into the back seat. A large woman, the same size and shape as Mary, leaned down and pointed her head into the car.

"Mrs. Castle?"

"Yes."

"Good. Right on time." The big lady slid gracefully into the Pontiac and creaked the heavy door closed with a loud slam.

We were in a very rough part of North Chicago. I didn't know it. I was six. Those six years had been spent sheltered up in the cozy North Shore suburbs. As I think back, my naivety would be exemplified by my memory of driving with my dad on a rainy night on the expressway, and an oncoming car did something to make him refer to the occupants. He referred to them as "colored folks." In my mind, at that moment I was picturing people with skin of all different colors. Faces with blue and red and yellow and some white. Colored people. Possibly the only African-American I had seen at that point of my life was Mary. In my mind, I still didn't know what colored people looked like. Mary was wonderful and this lady looked just like her.

Later when I found out that "colored" meant people with dark skin, I was confused as to why there was a designation at all. The blissful non-racist minds of children are precious.

Children start out with a clean slate. When I was five, at our summer cottage in Michigan, my sitter was a local Native American girl. My folks overheard me say to her, "Let's play cowboys and Indians. I'll be the cowboy. You be the Indian." Everybody laughed. I just wanted to be the cowboy. She thought it was funny. I didn't get it.

"Thanks for picking me up." The large lady let out a big sigh and turned in her seat to look at me in the back. An interesting new smell floated in the car. It was slightly familiar to me. It was very familiar to my mother, since she had attended many over-imbibed cocktail parties. "What a cute little boy. What's your name?"

"Cam."

"Oh, you are so cute."

I liked her. I knelt on the back seat and put my hands on the back of the bench seat so I could get closer. My mother pulled the car onto the street and started down the road. She turned right at the corner.

"Okay, little boy. Let's see how smart you are." She looked down at my little fingers perched on the top of the seat. "If you have ten fingers, and I chop three of them off with a butcher knife, how many do you have left?"

My mother turned right again, only much faster, kind of like how the limo sped forward after the shots rang out in Dallas.

"Seven!" I said proudly. I felt I got it right. I liked this lady. "Ask me another one."

My mother turned right again.

"Let's see . . ." She looked at my mother as we all leaned left in the car as she turned right for the fourth time, barely slowing down. The car screeched to a halt. "Hey, we're back at my house. That's odd."

"Ya know what? I just realized I had the wrong night. I cannot believe I made such a dumb mistake. Well, thanks anyways. If we need a sitter again, I'll give you a call. Okay. Thanks. Out ya go."

"Huh?"

"Mom? This isn't the wrong night . . ."

My mom reached all the way across and over the lady, yanked on the lever and gave the heavy door a fierce shove. "Thank you. Sorry."

The lady slowly got out. She shook her head. "Well. I never . . ." and closed the door.

My mom sped off.

"Mom? What happened? I liked that lady. Seven was right? Right?"

# Shut Up and Deal

"**C**ammie, it's past your bedtime. Go. We don't want to ask you again. We're really looking forward to this bridge game. Kim, go ahead and deal. Cammie, I don't care if you think you're not tired, get into that bed. Go!"

I remember standing there, looking at my mom, my dad, Kim, and my brother Steve, all happy as can be, seated around the card table. I wasn't tired. (No seven-year-old has ever admitted to actually being tired. Once, the first words out of my son Carter's mouth after I woke him up on the couch were, "I'm not tired.") I didn't want to miss out on the fun. But my mother's last "go" was pretty convincing, so I dragged my little body to bed, got in, and started muttering. "I'm not tired. I can't believe I don't get to . . .why can't I play? I am going to have to lay here and listen to them laughing and . . . *zzzzzzzzzzzzzzzz*."

As I slept, the four adults were having a grand time. Then the phone rang. Steve got invited out, excitedly accepted, and was out the door. Mom, Dad and Kim stared at each other in disbelief. They wanted to play bridge at that moment so badly but didn't know what to do. They needed a fourth.

So they decided to wake me up. Mom came into my room. "Cammie? Wake up dear. Remember how you wanted to play with us? Now you can."

"Wha . . .? Huh? I'm asleep. Go away."

"No, no, Cammie. Wake up. We need you. It'll be fun. Get up!"

Next thing I knew I was sitting at the card table, groggy, with three eager adults trying to give me a crash course on the game of bridge.

They gave me a cheat sheet with the order of the suits, notes on bidding, and the basic rules to playing cards and taking tricks. I remember struggling to hold 13 cards in my little hands without dropping them or showing them. "Keep your cards up! We can see them." It was a little overwhelming. I was tired, and after the first hand, I figured I had done enough and whined to go back to bed.

"Shut up and deal."

My mom said it mostly in jest, but also meant it. Dad and Kim laughed, and I dealt the cards. From then on "shut up and deal" was a family catchphrase that was often referred to over the years. It is used two ways: first, to describe a parent going back on or giving up on any form of discipline. And second, to refer to the act of forcing a child to mature before their years.

My young bridge expertise came into play a few years after that when our family was at our summer cottage at Northport, Michigan. Great Grandfather built the cottage in 1908 and the family has been going up ever since. It is on the Lake Michigan and rimmed by a golf course. Paradise. On one particular afternoon a number of families met at a large cottage on the lake. The adults set up three tables of bridge. The multitude of youngsters ran out on the rocky beach to chase seagulls and throw things. The adults added themselves up and, to much dismay, came to eleven.

"No problem. Cam can play. HEY, CAMMIE. COME IN HERE."

Soon I found myself with the grown-ups, seated at the felt covered card table, cards neatly sorted in my hands. All the adults were given the same beverage, a gin and tonic with a squeeze of lime and a glass swizzle stick. The host made twelve of them.

"I guess there's one for Cam. What's the harm? What the hell. Here you go."

I remember looking over my right shoulder, over my still effervescing cocktail, through the huge picture window, and out to the dozen or so kids near my age frolicking on the beach. I caught the eyes of some that had stopped their playing to stare back at me sitting at that table with the adults. It was such an odd mixture of acceptance and exclusion at the same time. I was proud to be sitting there, but feeling strange for not being with my cousins and friends. I don't remember exactly how I felt at that moment, but I do remember what I said. "One no-trump."

I wasn't always drinking cocktails before I was thirteen, sometimes it was wine.

It was common for my mom to come home from work, hungry, no food in the house and no money to buy any anyway. So? "Let's go out. I'll write a check." One of our favorite restaurants was . . . I'll call it The Village House since I am going to give away its secret. Forty-some years later, but better safe than sorry.

We would pull into the parking lot of The Village House and have trouble finding a space among the hundred or so cars parked in it. We would walk through the big front doors, turn right past the huge carpeted staircase leading up to two closed doors, and over to the hostess stand. There we would be greeted with a smile and escorted by the hostess into the very large and fabulously decorated dining room. Glass chandeliers hung from the ceiling. Thriving green plants were about. Linen tablecloths. We would be seated in the center of the room at a nice table for two. Two things were interesting about that. We always sat at the same table, and we were always the only people in the dining room.

"Mom? Where is everybody?"

"What? What people? Do you want a steak? I can't decide. Should I have the sirloin or have the filet? Put your napkin in your lap."

"Mom, there are a hundred cars in the parking lot, and we are the only ones here. Again."

"I feel like a having salad tonight. Do you? The blue cheese dressing here is very good. Oh, here she is. I think I will have the filet tonight. And a baked potato. Also a small salad with blue cheese. Cam? Do you want the same? Oh, medium rare. I would like a gin and tonic. Cam, would you like a glass of wine? Cam would like a glass of Burgundy. Thank you."

The waitress would bring me a glass of Burgundy wine, no problem. I was twelve. I would be sitting there at the table with the linen tablecloth touching my legs, polished silverware, a glass of red wine, and I would be reading my *Man From Uncle* book.

Later I learned from my dad what the deal was. Upstairs was the illegal casino. Also the favorite haunt of the local law enforcement. Up the stairs, secret knock I am sure, and bingo! Only no bingo. Black jack, roulette, quite the layout my dad said. That is why the waitress served a twelve-year-old boy wine. All the cops were upstairs at the craps table.

The dichotomy of my childhood with regards to maturing too fast and still staying a kid sometimes went the other way. The opposite memory of sipping a gin and tonic at the bridge table while the other kids played on the beach was an afternoon with my best friends, Mase and David, at Mase's house when I was thirteen.

The three of us in Mase's huge house. Mase had a basement fit for a prince. Ping pong table, real arcade pinball machine, tons of things to play with. I was always into army men, and Mase had the best and biggest collection. I wanted to play army men.

I was on the carpet. David and Mase were sitting on the couch. I said, "Let's play with army men."

What happened next has stuck with me for over forty years and counting. My two best friends, side by side on the couch, each with an ankle across a knee and one arm on the back of the couch. Leaning back as they spoke, the image was only missing warmed snifters of brandy. Their voices in unison, suddenly in low vibrato, they said, "Cam, we don't play with army men anymore. We're too old for that."

I remember two reactions simultaneously crashing into my young head at that moment. First being, "I am so embarrassed. I am so un-cool. My best friends have grown up without me." And second, "I can just play with army men when I get home."

So the question that needs to be answered here is, does being thrown into situations where one has to grow up faster than one is ready, having maturity thrust upon oneself, is that detrimental to a child, or is it a valuable leaning experience? I want to answer that right here with a resounding "maybe," because, I actually have no idea.

As I have raised my kids, I have I tried to not make the same mistakes. But once I saw no harm in showing my son Max when he was ten, the classic murder mystery by Brian de Palma, "Body Double." Twelve years later Max asked me while we were playing gin rummy, "Dad, why did you show me that soft core porn movie "Body Double" when I was, like, ten?"

And I said, "Shut up and deal."

# Like Running Downhill with Your Mouth Open

**W**henever my grandmother would serve my grand-father, Duffy, his favorite dessert, Snow Pudding, he would take one bite of the fluffy concoction and say, "Bessie, this is so good it is like running downhill with your mouth open."

I heard that expression a lot when I was young, living at home with Mom.

I always think of my mother as Lucy in "I Love Lucy", but she also is a tad like Peter Pan. She has always looked younger than her age and has devoted most of her waking moments to having fun. Often her strate-gies to achieve her goals were nuts, but the desire was the same. She has somehow retained the qualities that make youth joyous. When every other person neared adulthood and realized it was time to get serious and be practical, my mom was too busy plotting the next exciting escapade to look up and notice.

People often remark that I look younger than I am. When they ask me why that might be, besides pretending to blush and say, "oh, not really," I say, "I think it's because I am always smiling."

When you're taught every day of your young life that what you are experiencing is funny and fun, it's hard to not always be smiling.

For instance, my mother, my sister and I went on a Saturday shopping adventure when I was ten. We were on a quest to find foam rubber to stuff the pillow covers my sister had decided to sew. I have now, as I did then, no idea why she decided one day to sew her own pillow covers. It was not her usual style, but having made them, she needed to stuff them. I was forced to go along. It was a miserable choice of activity for a ten-year-old boy on a sunny summer day. I would have much preferred activities that would have resulted in a baseball traveling great distances, but instead I was in the back seat of our beige Pontiac, driving endlessly around the suburbs north of Chicago.

We did not let our fingers do the walking like the Yellow Pages ads incessantly begged us to do back then. No, we drove randomly around, stopping at any store that might have foam rubber. My sister and my mother didn't think it would be any challenge at all, especially if it were to result in a challenge that would, in turn, result in ending up in lots of different stores. They kept explaining that to me.

"This is called shopping. Shopping. It's fun."

I would reply, "No. It isn't. It is stupid." But we kept having the same exchange because, as I'd start to open my mouth to complain, they would simultaneously announce, "Well, no foam rubber here. Let's try a different store." They'd turn on their heels, grab my sleeve, and march to the exit. One store happened to also have a feeble section of sporting goods. I remember being thrilled to see items that actually interested me. They had baseball bats. Just as I started to wrap my little fingers around the handle of, possibly, a fabulous bat, I heard the stereo announcement that there was "no foam rubber here!" and I was yanked whining to the car.

Even they started to finally tire after what seemed like a dozen failed attempts. We were driving down the road, and we were all hungry. The fun, I suspected, had worn off for them. They were starting to get a little cranky, and snap at each other, when . . .

Up ahead, on the left, as we were barreling down the highway, among many large lit-up signs, were fourteen three-foot by three-foot letters stacked on top of each other announcing the name of this huge store. The letters spelled:

F

O

A

M

R

U

B

B

E

R

C

I

T

Y

There it was. Mecca. Music played. Our quest was to be realized. My mother swerved into the parking lot, slammed on the brakes halfway into a space, and we all jumped out. Giddy, slaphappy really, we ran to the big, glass double doors and swung them open. There was a salesman standing right there, eager to help us and amazed at our enthusiasm.

"May I help you?"

My mother said, "You bet you can." She cleared her throat, looked at both of us, and, using all the restraint available, said with a low voice and a poker face, "Do you have any foam rubber?"

"Foam rubber?" The salesman looked at my mother like she was crazy. "You mean just foam rubber?"

"Yeah, like to stuff a pillow with."

"No. We sell foam rubber furniture here. The furniture has foam rubber in it. We don't sell just . . . foam rubber."

With our shoulders slumped, we dragged ourselves back to the car. We got in quietly, turned to each other, and laughed. We laughed. I think that is as hard as any of us have ever laughed.

"If you can't find foam rubber at Foam Rubber City, I guess you just aren't going to find it," said my mother. "Let's head home."

So rather than a memory of the lousiest five hours of that summer when I was ten, I have the memory of one of the biggest laughs of my life.

My sister, by the way, threw out the pillow covers.

Whenever I was with my mother and things were going really well, or we had just taken a bite of something delicious, or found ourselves in someplace that was beautiful, or the weather was perfect, she would always turn to me and say, "You know what, Cammie? This is just like running downhill with your mouth open."

# My Mother and My Halloween Costumes

**B**y the time I came along, the last of my mother's four children, my mother was not quite as inspired about the motherly holiday child projects. My mother for so many years had been quite imaginative and dedicated to creating special holiday memories for my siblings. But I, being 13, 11 and 8 years younger than my brothers and sister respectively, my mother was, you could say, running out of gas. Don't get me wrong, she showered me with love when I was little and treated me wonderfully, but she wasn't going to spend time creating a Halloween costume. Turns out the one holiday she never cared for was Halloween.

I asked my siblings about their Halloween costumes through the years. "Ghosts." Lots of ghosts.

"What about that fairy princess costume with all the sequins? That was quite elaborate," I asked my sister.

"That? My friend Gloria's mother made it."

Some holidays, though, inspired our mother's amazing creative ingenuity. One Christmas, before I was born, my mother got the idea of an indoor/outdoor tree. There was a big picture window looking out to the front yard and the street. Outside in front of the window was a big brick planter box. She bought two Christmas trees and chopped the branches off one side of both of them and put one in a stand against the window on the inside and one in the planter against the window on the outside. She decorated both, and it looked from the street like the tree was growing through the window.

But, as I said, she was rather uninspired about holidays when it was just the two of us living together. Years after the amazing Christmas tree, for Easter, for example, I had to hide my own Easter eggs.

So, I was in first grade, it was the day before Halloween, and I said to my mom, "What am I gonna be Mom? I need a costume for tomorrow. Do you have one for me?"

"Hmm. Ah . . . you should have mentioned this earlier. I'll go to the store. It'll be fine. I'll be right back."

She returned and proudly handed me a thin cardboard box with a cellophane window, and in it, Fred Flintstone. The next morning I put that flimsy, plastic leopard skin bag over my body, and with great trepidation, I walked to school. I didn't know the word trepidation when I was in first grade, but if someone wanted to know what that word meant, all they would need to do is see the picture of me dragging myself through the backyards, in that costume, on my way to Avoca Grade School in that ridiculous outfit, holding my too big, can't see or breathe through, plastic Fred Flintstone mask, to understand the word.

When I got to school and noticed there were a lot of kids slumped over with bowed shoulders barely keeping their poorly fitting store-bought costumes from falling on the ground, I felt a little better. That was until the big voice out of the mesh circle near the clock told us to get in line and prepare to parade through the school and show off our "wonderful and creative costumes." That was the moment when the most obnoxious and annoying, larger than me, *girl* cut in line in front of me, and with cooing delight said, "Look, I'm Wilma! You're Fred! Get it? It's perfect! We need to spend the whole day together. I always liked you. Wow! How neat. I'm Wilma and you're Fred! This is great."

I made a mental note to kill my mother when I got home.

So now it's a year later. Exactly a year later, and I realize I don't have a Halloween costume.

"Mom! What am I gonna be?"

"Well, you should have thought of that earlier! You can be Fred Flintstone again."

"No Mom, no."

"Here, put it on. It still fits, kind of."

There I was, in a slightly stretched out, plastic, leopard skin, kinda bent masked, year-old Fred Flintstone costume, and I'm not happy about it.

"I am sorry Cam. I promise. Next year I will make it special."

A year passed. It was Halloween night.

"Mom?"

"What? Oh, is it Halloween again? Shoot! Ah . . . your father is still at work. Let me call him. I promised you. Didn't I?"

She dialed the phone.

"Bob? Oh, great! You're still there. You need to pick up a costume for Cam. Yes. (Leaning away) Anything. Oh! But not Fred Flintstone! Anything. Just not that. Thanks. (Turning back.) You father will pick you up a costume on his way home. Don't worry."

"Great."

So, my father showed up. Late, but not too late. It was dark out, but there was still plenty of time to Trick or Treat. My mom says, "Did you get a costume?"

"Of course. And you wouldn't believe it. There was only one left at the store."

"Oh, no."

"No. No. There was only one. But look. It's Frankenstein!"

"Frankenstein!" I was so happy. I ran to my dad. Yeah. I grabbed the box and pulled off the top of the cellophane windowed Frankenstein costume box and flung it. And in that box . . . was a costume. And it was not Frankenstein. It was Fred Flintstone. Fred Flintstone! Someone had put Fred Flintstone in that box. There was no Frankenstein Monster. No. Just Fred Flintstone again. What kind of cruel joke is this? I thought. It's forty years later and I can still feel the jarring pain that rushed through my little body when I saw that stupid smiling face. Fred. Not Frank. No bolts in the neck. No scars. Fred. "Yabba dabba do! Ahhh!"

"Bob!" My mom yelled, hoping to pin three years of crappy disregard of my Halloweens on him for his blunder. "How could you possibly . .?"

"Ah . . . it was the last one. Ah . . ."

"Oh, never mind. Here, Cam, I'll tear up a sheet. It will be fine. You can go as a ghost or a mummy or something."

She ripped up a sheet and wrapped it around me. It was October in Chicago and snowing. So she had to wrap my very believable mummy costume, the ripped sheet, around my bulky, a little too big, olive green coat. My best friend Mase showed up to go with me around our neighborhood to Trick or Treat. He had sent away in the mail for a makeup kit. He was a decapitated, yet restored, Nazi officer, complete with uniform, bloody stitches, and wheat paste to slick back his hair. He looked spectacular. I looked like an idiot.

So off we went with our pillowcases to collect and transport the huge cache of candy that awaited us. Snow was lightly falling, and it was a wonderful night. I was with my best friend. Just the two of us, young and on our own. Free to just walk up to any house in the lovely subdivisions of the North Shore of Chicago and have door after door open up, and high quality candy tossed into or bags.

And, at every door throughout that beautiful snowy night, the door opener would look out at the two of us and say, "Wow! What a cool costume. A Nazi. How scary. Ah. What are you?"

And there I was. Standing there with my ripped strips of what was earlier probably a perfectly good sheet, hanging off my too big, gangly, olive green winter coat.

And I said, every time, because it always got a chuckle and deflected some of my humiliation, "Ah . . . oh . . . I got hit by a car earlier. I'm okay though. Can I have some candy?"

Years later, when my son Max was twelve years old, he asked me if we could go to a costume store and pick out a costume. We were in that car in two minutes flat. I let him wander about the store, and after a while, he pointed to a costume in the adult size section and asked if it might fit him. There was a helpful employee nearby, and when I felt confident that the bloody fingers coming out of his forehead and cheek were most likely made of latex, I asked if they had that costume in a size that might fit Max. Max went into the dressing room and returned minutes later. "Whaddya think, Dad?"

"Fine by me."

I gladly plunked down $52.50, and we were on our way. Max was very happy and could hardly wait to show off his costume. My first choice would not have been this, but he was thrilled to be a pink, velour-clad, floppy-hatted, chain dangling pimp. Yup, my 12-year-old son was a pimp for Halloween that year. And one other thing is a sure bet. He wouldn't, under any circumstances, have to be that the next year.

# My First and
# Last Detention

**G**rowing up with a crazy mother has two benefits. It is never dull, and sometimes zany, impulsive antics can have beneficial results.

The first time my mother moved without telling me, though only a left turn, seven-house alteration, we crossed over the school district line. I went from walking to school, to being the first one on, and the last one off the bus that took me to Bell Elementary School in Wilmette, Illinois.

Basically, I was a well-behaved kid at school. I tried to follow the rules and never looked to get in trouble. Trouble can find *you* though. So, one day in fifth grade, Ms. Adler took huge offense in the hilarious time a fellow classmate and I were having. She gave us detention. My first one.

I brought the slip home and waited for my mother to get home from working at Marshall Field's in downtown Chicago. She worked hard at that job. It was exhausting for her because part of her character makeup is that if she is going to do something, she is going to go all out. Everything, no matter how small, becomes a project. A project that she is going to complete in a better and more unusual way than has been done before. If not, why do it? If it's planning a party, planting a flower, buying a blouse, or helping a customer pick out an item, she will put more effort into it than anyone else. Unless, of course, the project is something like moving, buying or selling a house or car, or getting a divorce; those are done spontaneously.

One day while working at Marshall Field's, my mother was sure she spied a shoplifter. She followed her through the store. When the very large woman went into the stairwell, my mother followed her, yelled for help, and cornered her on the stair landing between floors. All she had at her disposal as a weapon was the small nail file attached to her chrome nail clipper. She pointed it at the scary woman and snarled at her until security came.

"No big deal. She was a shoplifter. We caught her," she said when she got home. She said it with a happy lilt in her voice.

But most evenings she came home exhausted. When she came home from work, after fighting the rush-hour traffic, she was spent. I, on the other hand, always spent the three hours before she got home sitting on the couch, watching the Cubs game. Normally I would ask her, while still lying on the couch, "What's for dinner?" I often managed to get that question out before she even laid her car keys on the TV. The response was often just a tired grunt of, "I don't know yet."

One time, though, her response surprised me. Not to the point, of course, of changing my routine of coming home, lying down, doing nothing, and then popping the dinner question before she was all the way in the door. But it did surprise me.

"Dinner? Dinner? I'll show you what's for dinner!" She marched past me and into the kitchen. I heard cabinets open, pans clank, cabinet doors slam and then a shrill cacophony of banging metal.

Uh, oh. I ran into the kitchen, and my mother was sitting on the kitchen floor with her legs splayed out, a pot handle in each hand. She was pounding them on the floor in a rhythmic frenzy like a large version of that wind-up monkey with the cymbals gone mad. The pots were destroyed. Her hair was a mess.

She finally stopped, exhausted. She looked up at me and said in an eerie, slow, calm voice, "Why can't you wait until . . . why can't you just let me get . . . why can't you at least let me get my goddamned girdle off before you ask me about dinner?"

So, the day I brought home the detention slip, I didn't watch the Cubs game, I was up off that couch way before she got home. I might have even vacuumed. I was standing in the middle of the living room, smiling, when she opened the door.

"What have you done? Are you in trouble?" She darted her head around. "What is it? Is it bad news?"

"No, no, Mom, it's nothing. No, really, it's nothing. It's not really anything. Well, it's not that bad I mean . . . nothing. Nothing happened. How was your day?"

"That does it. What did you do?"

"I got a detention."

"That's all? Oh, I thought you had done something terrible, or someone died. No big deal." Then she went into her bedroom. A few minutes later she came out.

"There, once I get that girdle off, everything is better. What would you like for dinner?"

"Here, you have to sign this."

"What did you do?"

"Jeff and I were laughing."

"Laughing? You got in trouble for laughing? Hell, when I got detention it was for . . . well, it was for a lot worse things than that. Hey. If you go to detention, won't you miss the bus? How will you get home? You couldn't possibly walk. And I sure as hell won't get home in time to pick you up. I have an idea. Give me that note."

She went off to the kitchen, the bathroom, then my bedroom. She returned a short time later with a fully stuffed grocery bag in her arms with the note taped to the front. "Here, give her this." She handed me the bag.

I looked in the bag. On top was a baggie with my toothbrush, toothpaste and a comb. Under that were my pajamas, bulky flannel ones I rarely wore. The note read:

"I understand my son is being disciplined with detention after school. I respect and support your decision. This will result, of course, in Cam missing the bus. Seeing as Cam lives the farthest from the school of any student, walking home is not an option. I work downtown and will not be able to pick him up. So, I have sent with him his pajamas and toothbrush, because, if you keep him for detention, he will have to spend the night. Thank you. Dorothy Castle."

"Give that to your teacher and see what she says. Now, what should we do for dinner? Should we go out? I get paid soon. Let's go to Stouffer's. I'll write a check."

I went to school with the bundle and set it politely on Ms. Adler's desk. "My mom wrote you a note." Then I went to my desk and sat down.

With a few minutes left in the day, Ms. Adler walked up to me and handed me the bag. "I guess you don't need to serve your detention today. But I expect much better behavior from you going forward."

"I promise, Ms. Adler."

# My Mother and a Ticket

One evening about 10 o'clock there was a knock at the door of our little white house. I answered it. Standing on the doorstep was a police officer, a tall and intimidating figure. He was shaking a set of car keys in his right hand.

"Mom?"

My mother came to the door and said, "Yes?"

"Ma'am, is that your car out there, parked in front? That yellow Mustang?"

"Yes."

"Your keys were in it."

Taking them from him, "Thank you."

"That's against the law, Ma'am. Here," and he starts to hand her a ticket. "The fine is fifty dollars."

"WHAT? ARE YOU NUTS?"

"No, Ma'am. Your car could have been stolen."

"How did you find that I left my keys in my car?"

"I shined my flashlight in the car and they . . . twinkled."

"TWINKLED! That car is parked on my front yard of my property. How dare you give me a ticket? Why aren't you out fighting crime? I'm sure there are a lot more sinister things you could be spending your time and our taxpayer's dollars on, rather than lurking around peeking into people's private property. A fifty-dollar ticket? I'm not taking it!"

"Ma'am, you don't have the choice of not taking it. You can contest it to a judge if you like. Just check this box and send it in."

Snatching the ticket out of his hand, she said, "Oh, you bet your life I'm going to contest it. Why don't you go now and find some real criminals to harass. This is ridiculous. Now get out of my house!"

He stepped back, and she slammed the door. She looked slowly at me. She paused with a stern grimace on her face. Then a very slight smile started to appear.

In the courtroom the bailiff called my mother's name and told her to approach the bench. The judge said, "You have been charged with leaving your keys in an unlocked car. How do you plead?"

"I'll tell you how I plead. This is how I plead!"

She then proceeded to tear the notice of her court date into pieces and throw them in the judge's face. She turned around and stalked out of the courthouse.

She was so proud. She had stood her ground and showed the Cook County court system what she thought of their ridiculous laws and the misuse of our resource of taxpayer funded civil servants. She walked around like a proud peacock and told everyone she came in contact with about her victory in court. She was able to proudly relay that story for the whole month it took the $250 Contempt of Court citation to arrive in the mail. A citation she promptly paid. And only she and I were the ones who knew of this slam on the proletariat. We kept it our secret. And she smiled that slight smile again and whispered, "It was worth it."

# What's In a Name?

**M**y mother's name is Dorothy Dodo Dawn Judith Taylor Rose Castle Udovic. Let me tell you why.

Simple actually. Dorothy Judith Taylor was married three times and acquired two nicknames along the way.

When Dorothy was little, her parents were very impressed with a young athletic boy whose family belonged to the country club. His name was Douglas. His nickname was Dodo. My mom's parents thought that was a cute name and decided to refer to Mom by that. Dodo stuck. It stuck so soundly that for forty years or so, that was her name. She hated it.

To my mother, Dodo was the bird, the extinct bird that became that way because they were so easy for humans to do away with. Basically, one just had to walk up to a dodo and club it. And since one could, they did, over and over again. As the last one was beaten to death, humans remarked, "Boy, that is a stupid bird."

Shame the remark wasn't more like, "Those are awfully trusting and sweet animals. Maybe we should stop hitting them with clubs?"

In school, my mother's nickname of Dodo was often extended to be "Dodo Bird." She really hated that. Somehow she kept the name. To friends and family, referring to Dodo never conjured up images of possibly stupid birds, but rather a vivacious and kind person.

She used to wear a lovely gold necklace given to her as a gift. It was most likely rather pricey, being gold, and my mother wore it often. On the chain was her nickname. "DODO." The only trouble with the necklace, and I don't recall anyone other than me ever mentioning it, was that the "D's" were slightly rounded. Making it actually read "OOOO."

Maybe that is why, while wearing the necklace, no one ever asked about the name Dodo. Instead they just thought she wanted to wear a necklace that exclaimed, "Look at that!"

One day my mother and I were sitting at the dining room table at the house on Arbor Lane. I was about sixteen. We were having a casual conversation after some sort of small meal. The phone rang. I pushed back my chair, stood and took two steps to the open kitchen doorway, reached around the corner, and grabbed the phone with the very long curly-Q cord. My mom was at the head of the table dabbing away at the last bits of her food.

"Hello?" I said. "Don? No, there's no Don that lives . . ."

My mother and I are in complete agreement on what happened next. About what happened after that, we will never agree.

Before I could finish my statement explaining no Don's, my mother leaped, arms out-stretched, flying really, over the corner of the table to grab the phone.

She was airborne, and she was screaming, "I'm Dawn! I am Dawn!!"

This is where the cohesion of the story falls apart. Not over what she screamed next, but with regards to the guy on the phone. We both can still hear in our aural memory banks her yelling. "I'm Dawn! That's me! How could you be so stupid? I changed my name. That's a man I met at Parents Without Partners. How could you make such a mistake?"

"When did you change your name?"

"Recently."

"Why wouldn't you tell me? How was I to know?"

"Why wouldn't you ask?" She is still yelling at this point.

"Ask what? 'Just a moment, Sir. Hey mom, just wondering, you didn't change your name to Don recently, did you?'"

"That's just stupid."

At this point I have obviously hung up the phone. But I contend he called right back. She had given him her number, and he most likely would figure he dialed wrong and try again. I feel that is what transpired because I can, as clear as if it happened last week, see and hear my mother transforming from a screaming, sputtering, mad-woman into the most coy and adorable single woman in Chicagoland.

"Hello, I am Dawn. Oh, how nice of you to call."

My mother is convinced I hung up, and the guy never called back. She is adamant that she never spoke to him. She can prove it, too. "If I spoke to him, we would have gone out. If we had gone out, I would have married him. And I am pretty sure I never married him. SO, I never spoke to him."

With logic like that, it is a wonder I just didn't give up. But one of my strongest memories depicting my mother's broad array of talents was her ability to switch gears in mid-scream, to transform so instantaneously and convincingly before my very eyes. I was full bore into acting classes at that time. And I knew I would never be good enough to pull off something like that.

So, we don't agree. But since I'm the author, I win.

Her other three names are from her husbands. The last being Rudy Udovic. He was an interesting fellow who looked very much like Humphrey Bogart. He also was a scratch golfer who spent an inordinate amount of time on the golf course. That fact precipitated the stuffing of his likeness created to join my mother during the many dinners the real Rudy missed while still on the course. That scene is depicted in the photo on the front cover.

Just recently, when I showed my mother the proof of the back cover, she said, "I am not Dorothy Castle. I am Dawn Udovic. Nobody here at Emerald Heights will know who that is."

"But, Mom, through most of my life, you were Dorothy Castle. Throughout the book, you are Dorothy Castle, not Dawn Udovic."

"Look, Cam, I hated the name Dorothy, and I divorced the Castle. I am Dawn Udovic."

"Okay, Mom, I have an idea. For the copies that your friends at Emerald Heights want to buy, I will get and put on a sticker over Dorothy Castle so they will see your name as you like it."

"Oh, that is silly. You know what? Just because I am 93, it doesn't mean I am too old to change. Go ahead and put any name you want on the back of the book. It's your book, for God's sakes. Do what you think is best." Then we hung up.

I turned to my wife, Laura, who was standing near me. "Imagine that. She gave in." And I let out a big sigh.

One minute later the phone rang.

"Hi, Cam. I've changed my mind. Go with the stickers. Love you. Bye."

# My Mother and
# My Friends

**M**y mother loved my friends. I could have sworn she liked them all more than she liked me. That was probably not true, but it did make for the fact that all of them, in my mother's eyes, could do no wrong. That also meant she would do anything they suggested. She was incredibly accommodating to me and my friends. She would drive us anywhere. She would cook us meals at the drop of a hat. She would take us to the liquor store and buy us Mateus wine. Oh, wait, that sounds bad, a mother buying her son and his underage friends, liquor. But she had really, very good intentions.

You see it was 1970, and the hippie culture was still upon us, and she feared we would smoke pot or take drugs. So if she bought a harmless bottle of that sweet wine to split among us, we would refrain from the cultural pressures to experiment with "drugs." So she bought us the wine, and we were always so thankful, because, after smoking pot, our throats would get dry and that wine was just the ticket.

One night after a party broke up, a bunch of us realized that none of us had a ride home.

"Hmm. I know. I'll call my mom. She'll be glad to pick us up and drive us home."

So I called her. I think I woke her up since it was 2:30 in the morning. But I explained we were stranded, and she was willing to help us out. She showed up a little while later, and we were so grateful. We got ready to load ourselves into the car to be driven by my sleepy mother, in her long, light blue, quilted housecoat, to our respective homes scattered about the North Shore suburbs of Chicago. The interesting thing was, though, her car was a really cool yellow 1968 Ford Mustang, and there were nine of us. Some of our group were broken hearted that she showed up in this little car and wondered how were we going to decide who got a ride and who didn't.

"What?" says my mother. "You'll all fit. No problem. You four in the back seat. Now, you two in the passenger seat. Okay. You two will have to sit in the trunk. Really it will work. Look, we'll just leave it up. I'll drive slow."

"What about me?" I asked.

"Oh . . . here. You're in the trunk, too. Perfect! Let's go."

And so we did. And it worked. And those of the group who had never encountered my mother before were endeared to her forever. And the ones who knew my mother really well didn't give the situation a second thought.

I was lucky to be included in a group of thirteen pretty hip kids who were kind of the core of a large group of, basically, hippies. We had long hair, dressed in faded jeans and T-shirts, wore sandals or tennis shoes, but we were clean. Back then we were judged on our shabby appearance, but come to think of it, we looked a lot like the kids working today at Abercrombie & Fitch. On some occasions we, just for the fun of it, would spend the whole night in the park. We would just hang out, discuss the war and take naps with our heads on each other's stomachs, looking at times like a giant Scrabble board.

One particular night, we were visited by the Schaumburg Gladiators. Schaumburg was a town a little rough around the edges. It was south and west from the cushy North Shore suburbs. Occasionally some teenage males from there would think it great sport to drive over and beat up hippie, rich kids. Thus, they were given the nickname.

Our group was happy laying on each other in the park attached to Bell Elementary School late one evening, when five loud cars tore around to the back of the school and screeched to a halt on the blacktop. Twenty or so of the Schaumburg Gladiators spurted out of the cars and started snarling and pounding their fists.

"Uh, oh." I lifted my head off of Sally's gurgling stomach and assessed the situation.

"Ah . . . guys. I think we're all gonna die."

We all stood up with the alacrity of newborn fawns. Teetering and stumbling, we stood as a group, thirteen flower children, eight boys and five girls, dressed in frayed jeans, tie-died shirts, all with hair past our shoulders. In front of us were snorting, beer-infused, black boot clad rednecks. They had driven twenty miles on a mission to find some soft, anti-war, hippie offspring of supposedly wealthy North Shore Chicago parents, and beat the shit out of them.

Very much like Custer and his men, we knew we had no chance. Very unlike Custer and his men, we had no guns and ammo to at least prolong the massacre. We just stared at the angry group as they left their cars and marched toward us.

These guys looked like the cast of West Side Story, only it was about fifteen years after that movie was popular. We would have been laughing out loud looking at them, if *either* we didn't know we were about to die, or the drugs hadn't, hours earlier, worn off.

As they approached, the chivalrous instincts of the boys of our group started to take over. That was until the chivalrous boys remembered that we were tie-dyed, t-shirt wearing hippies with hair past our shoulders, and the two strongest people in our cabal were Sally and Julie.

The fist pumping, snarling males from Schaumburg marched closer. Then we all heard a sound. The quiet of this spacious park that lies behind the grade school and cornered by two main thoroughfares was only interrupted by the puttering of the still running engines of the gladiator's cars and the palpitating of our thirteen hearts. That is, until we all heard the deafening explosions of the engine of a Harley/Davidson motorcycle.

It came barreling across the grass and bouncing over the ruts in the field between the school and the gas station on the far corner. It skidded to a halt between the warriors and us. A big, solid guy, in his thirties, with thick blond hair and a beard, flung his left leg over the seat and landed, facing the enemy. He had a metal pipe in his hand.

"So, what are you all doin' here?"

"Who the fuck are you?" approximately twenty voices shouted in unison.

"I work right there." using his pipe to point. "That's my gas station. The real question is, 'Who the fuck are you?'"

One of their group stepped toward the guy with the pipe. "We're here to kick some hippie ass. What are you gonna do about it?"

"Well, I'm gonna stop you."

"Oh, yeah. There are twenty of us and only one of you, so what are you gonna do?"

"Well, I'm going to start by hitting each of you with this pipe." He walked toward their group.

They all took a couple of steps back. Then the apparent leader said, "Hey, you can't beat us all. There's twenty of us."

The guy with the pipe kept walking toward them, and, with a demeanor as calm as if he were ordering coffee, said, "Oh, I know I can't beat you all with this pipe. Really, all that matters to me is which one of you I get to hit first."

All the boys from Schaumburg scurried back to their cars. The supposed leader was shouting all sorts of confrontational things as he was backing into the passenger side of one of the cars. They squealed out of the parking lot and were gone.

The blond guy with the pipe turned around after it was quiet.

"Ah," one of us stammered. "Thanks. Ah . . . who . . . why . . .?"

"Oh, don't give it another thought. I like you guys. You don't mean any harm." He walked over and swung his leg over his Harley and started it up. He yelled over the banging engine, "I hate bullies." And he roared off across the bumpy field back to his gas station.

The Schaumburg Gladiators never returned. As a matter of fact, we never gave them another thought.

As long as we could see the lights on at that gas station.

Filled with new-found confidence, or simply pot-induced, shoddy memory, we spent many more nights in that park.

One morning, as dawn broke, some of the group declared they were hungry and how nice it would be to have a big delicious breakfast. Let's see. Six o'clock in the morning. No money. Breakfast?

"My mom will make us breakfast," I said.

"Great."

So we picked ourselves up from our lazy all-nighter in the park and walked the twenty-five blocks to my house. I opened the door and walked in. My friends stayed outside. My mom was asleep. I went to her door, knocked and opened it.

"Mom?"

"Oh, good morning dear. How was your night?"

"Great. Hey, I brought some friends home. They were kinda hopin' for some breakfast. Whaddya think?"

"Oh . . . ah . . . sure. Ah... let me splash some water on my face. What would they like? How about French toast?"

I went back to the front door. "Come on in."

They filed in, ten of my friends, at 6:45 A.M. They filed into our little white house on 930 Arbor Lane. My mother came out of the bathroom with a flourish. She was as alert as if she had been up for hours.

"Hi, everyone. Oh, look how many. Hi, Scott. Hello, Sally. Oh, David, how are you? Would everybody like French toast? You're supposed to put the bread out the night before, but I didn't know. It should be okay. Shouldn't take me too long. Does anyone want orange juice?"

And off she went into the kitchen at 6:50 A.M. and proceeded to prepare breakfast for eleven teenagers who had just spent the night in a park lying on each other's stomachs. And she's excited about it.

She served a wonderful breakfast. Everyone was very happy. And after the meal, we all just comfortably sidled into places to slip into a cozy nap. On the couch, the floor, my sister's twin beds, the twin beds in my room. Everyone was very content. And my mother was very pleased.

"What nice kids."

Later that year my friends Mase and David were over one afternoon. My mom was puttering about, and they were bored. Hmm. When they were bored, one of their favorite pastimes was to see if they could get me to overreact to something. They were sitting in the matching swivel, rocking, velour, tufted chairs on either side of the end table that held a big ecru lamp with a huge pineapple-shaped base.

\* \* \*

I must pause here. I mention that particular configuration because it was very important to me in my early teens. I often envisioned the table as a center and each chair as a guard and tackle of my offensive line that would block for me each time I turned into Gale Sayers. Gale Sayers was the star halfback for the Chicago Bears whom I would often transform into. Lining up behind the center, or table with lamp, I was no longer thirteen, and in a small living room in Glenview, Illinois. I was Gale Sayers. I would fake to the right towards the kitchen, jump left, receive the hand off, and cut around the left tackle, race through the hall, sail into my sister's room, leap into the air, and be brought down with a touchdown-saving shoestring tackle by my sister's bed.

I did this quite often, and got, what I felt was, extraordinarily good at it. So good that one day, when four friends-including two cute girls- came over to visit, I thought it would be a great idea to show it off.

I got in position and told the girls, Laura and Paula to watch me. What I didn't realize was the two boys, Scott and Dan, thought what I was about to do was ridiculous, childish, and downright embarrassing. To prove their point, unbeknownst to me, one positioned himself around the corner in the hall, the other behind the open door in my sister's room.

I barked "Hike" and was off like a flash. Two fakes and through the hall. That's when the one in the hall yelled "Now!", and the one behind the door slammed it shut. It's latched closed just as the top of my imaginary helmet blasted into it. The door smashed open, somehow not shattering the door frame, and I ended up on the floor. I was not sure what happened, but I did feel the knot on the top of my head start to grow. In moments it was the size of a large hotdog running from front to back on the top of my head. The two boys were in absolute convulsions of laughter. The girls were a 50/50 mix of compassion and pity.

My mother came into the room and saw me on the floor.

"Oh, for God's sake. Were you showing off to these girls with that stupid, phony football thing you do? Served you right. I'll get a dinner knife. Hold the cold blade to the swelling. Tsk. Tsk."

\* \* \*

So, now back to my bored friends, David and Mase, sitting in those chairs. They looked at each other. They didn't say a word to each other, but just stared, like they were communicating telepathically. Not like. They were. Then they both turned their heads slowly towards me and said, "Let's get your mom stoned."

"Huh?"

"Yeah." With sinister smiles and their shoulders tilted up, they both leaned towards me, and, with sardonic grins, they said, "Yeah, let's get Mrs. Castle stoned."

"No. No. Please. No. Come on you guys, don't"

And David, whom my mother described as a disciple of Christ, the boy she felt was a saint, the child who was the compassionate distillate of good, David, said, "Mrs. Castle?"

My mother entered the room.

"Mrs. Castle, would you like to try some marijuana?"

Now if anyone on the planet had asked her that she would have...who knows what she might have done. I had never ever considered the scenario. But from the mouth of David came the question . . . so her answer was, "Ah . . . ah . . . sure."

*SURE? Are you guys nuts? What are you doing? She's an adult. A parent. They are not even supposed to know pot exists, let alone know that we know what it is, let alone SMOKE IT THEMSELVES! SUPPLIED BY US! Are you guys trying to drive me crazy?*

*Yes.*

"Here, Mrs. Castle, sit down. Mase, hand me that joint. Okay, Mrs. Castle. I'm lighting it now. Take a big puff. Hold it in. Good. Now do another. There you go. Oh, coughing is normal. Whaddya think?"

"Gee, I don't feel a thing. You know this pot is not that big a deal after all. I don't feel anything. Well, thanks anyways you guys. I better get back to the dinner."

She went back into the kitchen, and I looked at my two ex-friends with an incinerating glare, and they laughed silently to themselves to the point that they might have ruptured something. And it was quiet. Then we heard a sound. It was coming from the kitchen. A very strange sound. It was a screeching sound. Faint, and then loud.

"E EE. EEE. EEEEEE."

"What the hell is that? What is that screeching sound?" all three of us thought.

"EEEE. EEE. EE. EEEEE."

It kept going on. Then it stopped. My mother came swooping out of the kitchen with a long trailing banner in her hands and said to David and Mase, "Excuse me."

They got up from the chairs, and she stood precariously on the left, rocking, swivel chair and proceeded to tape up her banner. She moved to the other chair and proudly finished displaying her creation.

What was now taped to our living room wall was seven feet of shelf paper that she had magic-markered on the backside with the words, in twelve-inch high florescent green letters, "THE LITTLE GRASS SHACK!"

Then she went right back in the kitchen without saying a word. The three of us just stared at this banner taped to the wall. A few moments later she yelled, "Dinner's ready!"

She served us roast beef and roasted potatoes, and it was very good. Mase and David could barely eat because they were still consumed with the all out laughter they had not yet been able to expel. And my mom was just chowing down. My mother has impeccable table manners and a very moderate appetite. But that night, as she was scarfing down her meat, Mase and David were just mesmerized looking at her. She looked up from her plate and said, "Food has never tasted this good to me. I don't know why. Hmm. David? Are you going to eat that potato?"

And before he could answer, she stabbed his potato with her fork and plopped it on her plate.

"You guys can smoke all the pot you want because it doesn't do a thing. I don't know what all the fuss is about. Anybody want some more of this roast?"

So my mother got stoned and didn't know it. My friends successfully freaked me out. My mother once again showed her graciousness when it came to my friends. And I did the dishes. The banner was still up the next morning, and my mother didn't admit she didn't quite remember completely why that was so appropriate the night before. But Mase called me the other day, thirty years later, and when I mentioned to him I was writing stories about my mom, he said, "Have you written the one about 'The little grass shack?'"

And I said, "Not yet."

# Mom and Pot

Actually, the first time my mom smoked pot was not right before she taped the Little Grass Shack banner to the wall.

Let me explain.

I was in high school from 1970 to 1974. Recreational drugs were so rampant they were part of the culture. It seemed very different back then. There was no such thing as crack. There were heroin addicts, and plenty of people dying from being one, but the basic, everyday drug use was borderline reasonable. Pot was so mild compared to today.

Tell me if this would happen now.

We were at a party, twenty or so of us, and nobody had any pot. Some people were quite anxious to have pot be part of their Friday night, but didn't know how to rectify the situation. One amazing, industrious fellow, who shows up in a number of chapters, but will remain nameless, at least for this page, found some pot that was available. Problem was it was many miles away and, this is painful to confess, no one had a car.

Quite possibly this was not because we were poor, but because we weren't old enough.

So, Mr. Resourceful rode his bike to get it. By the time he returned with it, it had been what seemed like hours. Noticing how frustrated the group was, he snapped his fingers, pointed his index finger in the air, and said, "I have an idea."

He found the phone book, tore a yellow page out of it, creased it in half, and then poured the entire one ounce bag of pot onto it. He rolled it up, lit it, and passed it around.

I have not smoked pot in decades, but the rapid pace at which its potency was increasing at the tail end of my experience with it, leads me to believe that, today, not only would such a stunt be cost prohibitive, but would hurt.

Part of the routine back then was to indulge in something, then try to make sure no adult or authoritative person knew that you had. Maintaining one's composure most of the time, while being high was part of the game. One classmate, my junior year in high school, announced at the beginning of the first semester that he was going to smoke pot every morning of the school year and still bring in a straight "A" grade average. He did it. Later, folks I knew who smoked pot every day, not only didn't get out and excel, but had trouble actually making it out of their basement on any consistent basis-like once a week.

Though my mother was different from most moms in almost every way, there was one way she matched up with most, the parental fear that "my child will end up on drugs." My mom was vigilant. The ironic thing was I was the last one of our group to smoke pot. My friends all started smoking pot when they were around 14 years-old. I waited, I resisted, because my mother did the meanest thing. She sent me out into the night with these cruel and hurtful words, "I trust you." Damn. When all my friends were being threatened or ignored, I was given complete freedom, with that horrible caveat.

"Where are you going at nine o'clock on a school night?"

"Tommy's"

"Remember, you do have school tomorrow?"

"Yeah, Mom."

"Well, don't stay out too late."

"I won't."

"Cam? It's okay. Because, you know, I trust you. Have a nice time."

The kiss of death, that trust. I had all the freedom I wanted as long as I didn't blow it.

So, each night I went out to be with my friends and had this ball and chain of trust I had to drag around with me.

The other thing was she was psychic. Her brain was so tied into my actions it was like she had a camera attached to me. One night I was lucky enough to be out with two of my ridiculously cool friends. And they were out to cause some trouble. We crawled out a basement window after curfew (70's, North Chicago suburbs, curfew? I have no idea why) and I followed them as they harassed other houses in the neighborhood. Suddenly, out of nowhere, a cop car came racing toward us, slammed on the brakes, skidded sideways, the door flew open, flashlight, and the policeman yelled, "Goose! Haynes! Who are you? Get in the car!" He had dealt with my friends so often he recognized them by their shadows. He was quite baffled by the fact he had no idea who I was.

The three of us got taken to the station and put in cells. I remember being fifteen and sitting in that cell. A toilet with no seat, and a cot. I sat on the cot just looking around at the bars and the dull, blank walls. This jail was in the soft suburbs north of Chicago. It wasn't filthy, and I didn't feel at all threatened, just bored. A little while later an officer came to my cell. "Come with me. You can go."

In the station were my mother and my sister. "Oh, Cam. Oh, Cam." A whole bunch of that, and then we left. In the car my mother was all dramatic and then she stopped abruptly. "You know what that officer said to us? That you were the most polite boy they have ever arrested. How about that? I am so proud of you."

Then she went on to tell what happened previously back home. My sister was back from college and sleeping in her room. Mom woke up from a sound sleep, went in to Kim's room, and woke her up. "Kim! Wake up. I can't sleep. I have never felt this before but I think Cam's in trouble. What do we do?" Right after that, the phone rang and it was the Wilmette Police department.

Shortly after that, since I now was a seasoned criminal, I gave in to the badgering of my friends to finally join them in smoking pot. Nothing kills the buzz more than one righteous moron sitting there not joining in with the group. I was still completely free, save for that tether of trust. My mom didn't look at the arrest as a negative. She was just proud of me for being so polite. So, we were all at Tommy's house. A school night. Ten o'clock. "Come on, Cam."

"Okay." We crawled up the steep ladder into Tommy's room in the attic, and with friends all a titter, someone started rolling a joint. As someone was getting ready to light a match, we heard a phone ring. Then at the bottom of the ladder was a figure most of us had never seen before, a very sleepy and confused figure. Tommy's dad. "Tommy? Do you have somebody up there named Cam? His mom's on the phone. What the hell time is it?"

"Yeah, Dad. He's here. No problem. Go back to sleep."

They all looked at me like I was an alien from another planet. If my irises, at that point, had narrowed into oval slits, they wouldn't have been surprised. I climbed down the ladder, and a very groggy man in boxers and a stained T-shirt handed me the receiver of a phone with about ten feet of cord. "Mom?"

"Cam. Glad I found you. I know I have never done this before, but, could you come home now? I just have this very funny feeling like you are about to do something wrong."

"Yes, Mom."

One Saturday afternoon my mother was doing the laundry. I was watching TV. She came into the room with a sly look on her face. "Cam. Come here."

I followed her. On the washer was one of my shirts. Next to it was a very small pile of black dust. "What is THAT?" She pointed it at it like it was damning photographic evidence in a murder trial. "I found this in the pocket of your shirt. It's pot, isn't it?"

I licked my finger, touched it to the evidence, and put my finger to my tongue. "Oreo cookie crumbs, Mom. Anything else bugging you?"

Completely defeated, she laid off for awhile. That conveniently coincided with me going full bore into the pot smoking thing. We had a ball. We would smoke it all the time. And, smoke it out of stranger and stranger devices. A potato. A toilet paper tube. My favorite was a "Proppa PH" bottle. (Clear, liquid, acne medicine that came in a tall, plastic bottle that was just the right shape and size for a bong.) Aluminum foil, tooth picks, and rubber bands were pretty much all you needed to turn these everyday items into working pipes. I was so proud of these I kept them behind my dresser. The dresser had a false bottom I could access from the back. Sliding the dresser on my black and white, linoleum tiled floor was a breeze. I could do it silently, so even if Mom was home, but in her room, I could retrieve my paraphernalia.

One afternoon, after school, I went into my room and slid back my dresser. On the wall was a skull and crossbones pirate flag nailed to it. I nearly fell over. My assortment of pipes and materials were still there, but that flag was pretty eerie.

It seemed like forever until my mom got home from work. I was sitting on the couch with a stilted grin on my face. She opened the door, slapped her keys on the TV, walked over and dropped a small, dark green bag on my lap. "Open it." It was a bag from Marshall Field's. In it was a corn cob pipe. "I saw what you smoke that pot out of. Disgusting. I figured I am not going to talk you out of smoking it, so . . . I thought if you are going to smoke it, you should smoke it out of something nice. I'm going to go change." And she walked into her room.

A few days after that, she was in her bed reading a book. I was talking to her about something, and she said. "Okay, I'm curious about what's the big deal with the pot. Do you have any? Go get it and let me try it."

I got some. "It's pretty subtle," I said. "Especially the first time. Here, take a puff."

She sucked in a little smoke, let it out, waited for a moment, and said, "I don't feel a thing. Smoke as much as you want."

After that, besides David and Mase getting her stoned, something she promptly, completely forgot about, pot was no longer a topic. I was extremely covert and she wasn't interested. She never really gave it another thought. Not even after eating the brownies my friends left in the kitchen one night when I was home from college. We thought the brownies were terrible, so we didn't eat more than a few bites and left them in the kitchen. Instead, we drank large amounts of a very tasty punch that had, among the ingredients, 151 rum. When we drug ourselves out of our respective beds the next morning, my mom was wafting about with a beaming smile on her face.

"Who made those brownies? They were so good I had three of them!"

## "Get a Job."

The day after the day my mother forgot my sixteenth birthday, she told me to get a job. That is not entirely accurate, she did remember my birthday, but not until Wendy and Laura came to the door at ten o'clock at night after I had spent the day of my sixteenth birthday wondering if anyone would remember.

They showed up at the door with a cake, party hats and their lovely selves to completely make my day, if not my year. That spurred my mother, realizing that she had truly forgotten her last child's monumental sixteenth birthday, to spring into action. That action being going to the only store open at ten o'clock on a weeknight in Glenview, Illinois, in 1972, the newly opened concept store called "Convenience." At least that's what I remember we called it.

What was convenient was that it was open. The charm of the store was pretty much that. It was open. I was very into records at that time. They *had* records. She came back while the girls were serving me cake and proudly gave me my gift. "I didn't forget your birthday. Here."

I pulled a record album out of the grocery bag. "The Ink Spots. Thanks, Mom."

"Oh, they are very good. Have you heard of them? Girls? Have you heard of The Ink Spots? They were very popular in my time. Happy Birthday."

So, the next night, one day after my mother basically forgot my sixteenth birthday, she came into the living room.

"Cam?"

"Yeah?" I was sitting in one the velour, swivel chairs that made up the left side of my imaginary offensive line. I had one of my legs over the arm of the chair and was bobbing slowly, watching TV.

"You need to get a job."

"Yeah."

"You just turned sixteen. You need to get a job."

"Okay."

"No. I mean now. You are old enough to work. We need the money. Go get a job."

"What? What are you saying? I'm watching TV." I kept bobbing. She was just glaring at me. "Fine. I'll get a job."

"You could work at Hackney's. That restaurant is so busy, I am sure they need some help.

"Yeah."

"Get up."

"Huh?"

"Stand up. I mean it. You are sixteen. Stand up right now and walk on down there. I mean it." She stood up, went to the TV, and bopped the palm of her hand on the knob of our big console RCA television set and turned it off. Then she turned and pointed at the door. "Go."

"You are serious."

"You bet I am. Get up and walk down there."

I got up. My mouth was open in complete disbelief that my mother was ordering me, with no prior warning, to go apply for a job at 9:45 at night . . . and I was doing it!

I went out the door and walked with shoulders slumped and my head down. My eyes were focused intently on the cracks in the sidewalk caused by the burgeoning roots from the giant old elm and oak trees that towered above the yards of our neighborhood, forming that precious arch, that beautiful canopy above those streets. I didn't appreciate the arch of those magnificent tree branches that night because I was focused intently on the cracks in the sidewalk pushed up by their roots.

I had no idea what I was supposed to do. I had no idea what to expect. I did not want to walk into that restaurant. I didn't really want a job. I was not dead set against it because, before about seven minutes previously, the thought had never entered my mind. I dragged my feet and stubbed my toes carelessly into some of the raised "Z"s of concrete, subconsciously hoping for a sprained ankle or broken tibia (got a "B" in biology), so I would not have to go through with this.

I made it to Hackney's on Harms Road. They were open and busy. The restaurant looked like a rustic house, with dark reddish-brown wood siding. The large fan atop the roof was billowing the aromas produced in the small kitchen. The pungent smell of their famous fried onion rings mixed with the usual aromas created by cooking mountains of French fries and hundreds of burgers to coax people in. I wasn't hungry.

I dragged my droopy shoulders through the door and was face to face with a cheery, cute girl at the hostess stand. Behind her was the noisy din of a busy restaurant: clanking dishes, the rumbling dishwasher, diners and drinkers muttering and laughing.

"One?"

"I think I want a job."

With the canker sore sweetness of a Sunny Delight or Tampax ad, she said, "The manager's right there at the bar. That guy. Talk to him."

I scuffed my way over to that guy at the bar and stood behind his right shoulder. He was sucking on an amber colored drink in a short glass and was shaking the ice cubes.

"What do you want?"

"I think I want a job."

"Great. Our dish washer quit tonight. Can you start tomorrow?"

"I guess so."

"Great. Come back tomorrow at four. I'll have someone show you what to do. Okay?"

"Okay."

Damn. I got a job. What a crappy bad turn of luck was that? I walked home in half the time it took me to get there.

When I walked in, my mom was standing in the middle of the living room with a sheepish look, tapping her fingertips together. "Did you get the job?"

"Yeah. I'm going to bed." I walked past her and into the bathroom.

I am pretty sure at that moment *her* mouth was open.

# My Mother and
# The Zoo Story

I went to New Trier High school north of Chicago. It was considered one of the best high schools in the country. Those of us who went to it never really could figure out why that was, but we were proud anyway. It was known for its theatre program. There were a lot of famous movie stars who went to New Trier: Ann-Margaret, Glen Ford, Rock Hudson, Bruce Dern, Charlton Heston and Ed Blachford. Okay, so Ed was in my class. But he was in a Sam Peckinpaw film where he had to eat a bag of pot. We were very proud of him.

I took theatre classes the entire time I was there. (Until my mother moved the second time without telling me.) In my junior year I was cast in the play "The Zoo Story" by Edward Albee. The play has only two characters in it. It's 65 minutes long. My lines consisted of 55 minutes. I was terrified. How would I memorize all of that? My co-actor was very good. To sit there on the bench and make facial expressions through the rehearsals and the performances for what was truly unending hours, and always stay in character, was remarkable. But he stunk! I'm sorry to say that if he is reading this now. But he stunk. Stunk! A putrid sickly sweet, rancid B.O. that I can still unfortunately remember today. I had to bend down close to him and say my lines for hours, smelling, that odor.

I practiced my lines during every waking moment. I was sixteen and had recently started my first job at Hackney's Restaurant.

So there I was, at the deep fat fryer, practicing my lines.

" . . . and she pushed me against the stairs, stinking of lemon-flavored gin. She tried to kiss me with those rotted teeth." The guy cooking the hamburgers next to me would just sigh. He got so sick of me spouting this crazy stuff. The play, by the way, is a bit out there. It's my character choosing someone at random on a bench in New York's Central Park and spending 65 minutes trying to convince this poor innocent (stinky) stranger to kill me. I would practice. And practice. And my co-workers wanted to stuff me into the deep fat fryer. But I got it down.

The first performance was for the group of students who were in the experimental Junior class I was part of. It was called "Humanities." They selected 100 students to participate in this new, unstructured, cutting-edge, experimental style of high school education. It was wonderful to be part of it because all 100 of us realized early on this was going to be a rich and different and unique learning experience that would end up requiring no effort on our part whatsoever. Also, by sheer luck, the cutest girls in the school were in it.

The morning of the first performance, I was terrified. How would I remember all those lines? My mother had asked if she could see this performance, and I had explained that it was the first one, it was just for my schoolmates, I was very nervous, she could see the regular performance the next night, and if she tried to sneak in and see this performance, I would remove some randomly picked, yet very important organ of hers with a spoon. She understood. She would see my long-awaited stellar performance later. Tomorrow. Sure. Her son. Her life and blood. The son she brought into this world. She would just wait until tomorrow.

That morning I was ready. I was so nervous, but was I dressed and alert and ready to get on the bus. My performance was at 8:00 A.M. My mom, because of my big day, was up early and made me a beautiful breakfast I couldn't eat. She was standing there in her long house coat. She gave me a hug, kissed me and wished me good luck. I got on the bus. I was relieved, because I knew how much my mother wanted to see my first performance. I had been so sure she was going to be unable to control herself and somehow mess it up for me. But, thank God, there she was. Home now, rinsing the maple syrup off my plate in her long quilted floral housecoat.

Yeah, sure.

As soon as the bus pulled out of sight, she unzipped her housecoat, underneath she was completely dressed. She slipped on her shoes, jumped in the car and sped off after the school bus. She showed up at school behind a dozen school buses (3600 kids went to my school), and she lost me completely. She started going up to kids and asking, "Do you know where The Zoo Story is? Do you know where The Zoo Story is?"

They looked at her like she was from Mars.

The performance was in a small auditorium that seated a little over 100 people. The stage was on ground level, and the seats rose up from there. There were two sets of big metal doors that opened into the room right behind the stage, so the audience had to go in and be seated before the actors could enter onto the stage.

My 100 classmates were seated, including the very cute girls. My stinky, yet capable, co-actor entered the auditorium and sat on the bench.

I paused. I collected my thoughts along with my 55 minutes of memorized lines.

*I am him. I am the character. I am Jerry. I am going to convince this poor soul to kill me. It's going to be great.*

I took a deep breath, pushed open the large metal door, and it slammed shut loudly behind me. I stepped onto the stage. The audience's eyes were affixed on me. I stepped across the stage. I looked down at the poor fellow on the bench, "I've been to the zoo. (Pause) I've been to the z . . ."

And at that moment the big metal door behind me opened up, the door that should not really be in anyone's suspended disbelief of New York City's Central Park, and through it walked my mother. She walked right past me. Onto the stage! I have 54 ½ minutes of lines left to emote from memory, and my mother just walked through our imaginary Central Park, past my stinky future victim and up the aisle. "Excuse me. Excuse me," she says, at last seating herself at the last and only empty seat at the top of the auditorium next to Cheryl with the wonderful, natural, long, wavy blond hair. With her purse clutched tightly to her lap, my mother waved at me, smiled really big, and mouthed, "I made it. Do really good."

I somehow composed myself and made it through. It went pretty well. My classmates enjoyed it, and I felt good about it. They clapped like crazy, and the cute girls looked at me like I was really cool. But I still wake up nights reeling at the sight of my mother standing on the stage next to me during the second line of my biggest performance.

And come to think of it, I never got any closer to Cheryl than she did.

# My Mother and a
# Boeing 747

**M**y mother and I were flying from Chicago out to Seattle to visit my brother, and we were on a big Boeing 747. We were in the last row, in the last two seats on the left hand side of the plane. It was a long flight. But it was okay. My mom and I were excited to be traveling, and we could hardly wait to visit my brother Truman and his family on our first trip to Seattle.

The flight was fine, the food surprisingly tasty, and we amused ourselves with our nervous banter. It was dark out so there was nothing to see out the window. But it was getting near the end of the flight, and we would be on the ground soon. The pilot announced that we were beginning our descent, and we should perform all the passenger duties. So we were buckled, upright, and our tray tables were right where they should be. The stewardesses (this was the seventies, no one had heard of flight attendants) had collected any lingering debris, checked our tray tables, and were strapped into their little seats. The plane started to lurch forward in its descent, and as the engines got louder, my mother turned to me and said . . .

Now, so far through this trip with my mom had been great. We got along and had fun. Which is not all that common between a parent and a teenage boy. My mother had been unusually calm and hadn't done one thing to embarrass me, something that was not hard to do, because she . . . is who she is. And I was a teenage boy. Teenage boys are easily embarrassed. I remember being awkward and feeling awkward as a teen. Some of my friends exuded great confidence, but I am pretty sure that many peers felt the same way as I. I remember walking through the lunch room feeling hundreds of eyes were on my and I looked foolish. When in reality, most likely nobody was really paying attention to me getting some more milk. So I was very happy that to this point on this trip, I had felt okay.

"My, God! We're in the last two seats on this plane!"

"Yeah?"

"Don't you see? We'll never get off this plane. We will have to wait until three hundred people get off. No way. Follow me."

"What?"

"Follow my lead. When I tell you, follow me. We have got to get ahead of all these people or else we will be on this plane forever."

"Huh?"

The big plane was plunging towards the earth. It was starting to level out. The sound of the engines was getting louder. The sounds of the passengers were getting fainter. My ears felt like there were drinking glasses cupped over them. The nose of the plane tipped up. The wheels under the wing screeched into the ground. And before the wheels under the nose of this huge hurtling behemoth touched down . . . my mother leaned over, unclicked my seatbelt and yelled,

"NOW!"

"What?'

"Now. Now. Go. Go. Go. Get up. Run."

"But . . . ah . . . Mom?"

She, from her window seat, stepped past me into the aisle, reached back and grabbed my arm.

"COME ON!"

With her pulling me, we were running up the aisle of a completely full Boeing 747 that was careening down a runway at a speed that has yet to be reduced to less than . . . I don't know how many miles per hour. All I know is that I could hear over the very loud noises that are produced by landing this giant metal machine, filled to the brim with people and stuff, the sound of two stewardesses screaming at my mother and me. And mom was pulling me. I have to admit, I was not as determined to get to the front of this plane as she was. As a matter of fact, I mostly felt self conscious to be 15 years old and in front of all these people staring at me as my mother was pulling me by the arm.

One of the screaming stewardesses unlatched her seatbelt and came bolting down the aisle. She grabbed me by my other arm and, through gnashing, clenched teeth, hissed, "Get back in your seats!"

I had my mom pulling one arm with the stewardess pulling on the other. In most situations my mother's determination always wins out. But she was no match for the stewardess's fury who was yanking on my other arm as we were lurching back and forth in the aisle as the speed of this giant plane was slowing rapidly to somewhere near 100 miles per hour. As my arm was pulled from my mother's grasp, she realized getting to the front of the plane without her son would basically defeat the purpose of her mission. So after a moment of considering the ramifications of leaving me behind, she dejectedly struggled behind me to get back to our seats.

The plane was just starting to come to the end of the landing and cozying into the process of taxiing on the tarmac, when we plopped ourselves back into our seats. The stewardess was holding onto two seatbacks and swaying back and forth as the plane turned to head for the gate. She was glaring at us. She was so mad she could not speak. She went back to her seat, flopped down, took a huge breath, and strapped herself in, ten seconds before she had to get up.

My mother was fuming.

"We would have made it. Why didn't you run? We could be at the front of the plane right now. But no. You had to hold us back. Great. Why can't you just be aggressive for once in your life? Now we will never get off this plane."

She was so mad at me.

I think about my oldest son, Mason, when he was 16 years old. If he were thrown into a situation where he would need to react quickly or follow spontaneous commands, he would react very much like Earl, our box turtle. If I were to have yelled at him to hurry, he at that moment would have taken a posture that would very much resemble, and has all the urgency of, an old growth cedar tree.

We made it off the plane finally. And we were the last two off, just like she said. But immediately upon getting off that plane, just like always, this episode was past and it was on to the next. So now her focus was finding our luggage and setting off to visit her first-born son, Truman. She was happy now and excited. And I was still very embarrassed that I was yanked back to my seat in front of 300 people by an irate stewardess. But once again my embarrassment was quickly washed away with the one recurring thought that always makes it all okay.

Someday, this is going to make a good story.

# My Mother and Returns

**M**y mother is the World Champion, Gold Medal winner when it comes to returning things she has purchased or been given. Her talent and extensive resume are unmatched. She has the natural attributes of being clever and cunning, and, at the drop of a hat, endearingly charming. Add to that the ability to strike like a cobra at an unaccommodating and out-matched customer service person who might not realize they are dealing with an Icon. She is undefeated in the arena of returns.

Another reason my mother is so good at this is because she has had a lot of practice. She has had a lot of practice because, in looking back over her life, if one were to take all the things that were given to her, and most of the things that she has bought for herself, and put them in a pile, and then take all of those things that were returned by her, and put them in a pile, the piles would be the same. That is because out of those things given to her or purchased by her, she has returned . . . all of them. Okay, so I'm exaggerating. She still has the small diamond shaped terrarium I gave her that is in her living room. And I think she still has the little stained glass, cardinal bird candleholder I gave her, on her windowsill. But that's it. My siblings are a tad ticked off that they are both from me. But that's it. So the material I have to work with for this story is nearly everything ever acquired by my mother.

I will only mention a few of the gems.

She returned paint. Oh, not paint still in the cans. No. She returned paint that was already dried on the walls of our living room. Now this doesn't qualify for the A list because technically she didn't get her money back. But it's the perfect example of her uncontrollable desire to not keep what she has just bought.

We were living in the house at 334 Willamette Avenue in Glenview, Illinois. Mom, Dad, two brothers, my sister and a very young me all lived there. Thinking about that house brings to mind many stories of our mother's uncontrollable spontaneity. For example, one morning my father was going out the kitchen door to the garage to drive off to work in downtown Chicago, when he stopped, looked back at my mother and said, "You know, I have always wanted Dutch Doors." And he headed off to work.

That's all Mom needed. She got up from her cup of coffee, took the door off the hinges, plopped it on the dining room table, got a saw out of the garage and sawed the thing in half. She went to the store, bought the necessary hardware, hung the two pieces back on the hinges, and that was that. So when Dad got home that night, he turned the knob on the kitchen door, pulled open the bottom half, and nearly knocked himself out on the still closed top half of his brand new Dutch Doors.

This was about the same time Mom decided she wanted to have the living room painted a new color. She talked Dad into agreeing to pay for it and told him green would look very nice. A nice light shade of green.

She arranged for the painters to come in, picked a color, and in one day and for $250, the living room was transformed into a soothing soft green room, begging to be relaxed in. Dad came home and remarked that it was very nice and sat down in his chair and read the paper.

The next morning Dad was off to the grinding commute to Chicago and another stressful day in the office. After he left, Mom stood in the living room and looked around, with one hand cupping her chin and the other cupping her elbow, pondering ala Jack Benny.

"It's too dark! I don't like it. It was supposed to be lighter." She went to the phone and called the painters.

"Hello, this is Dorothy Castle. You painted my house yesterday. Oh, no, you did a fine job. It's just that . . . it's . . . ah . . . it's too dark. Could you lighten it up? Is that possible? Another $250? Ah . . . that's fine. Could you do it today? Great. Oh, one other thing. Could you be done before six o'clock?"

They did. And it was a tad lighter. And Mom was very happy.

Dad came home not long after the tarps, brushes, pails and painters were hurriedly loaded on the truck and gone. He sat down in his chair and started reading the newspaper. He stopped and peered over the top of the paper and looked slowly around at the walls of the comfy room. My mother was standing in the room, looking at him, tapping her fingertips together in front of her chin, with quite a quirky smile. Nothing we haven't seen before. Dad thought for a minute, then shook his head and muttered, "nah." Sure he was crazy, he went back to his reading. It worked. He didn't notice.

That was until he got the bill from the painters for $500.

A few years ago my mother went to a movie by herself. She bought her ticket, found her seat, and as the never-ending previews started, she realized she was cold. Why, by the way, is it that movie theaters feel compelled to make the temperature in the theater the exact extreme opposite of the temperature that's outside? If it's summer and sunny and hot out, you had better pack a sweater because the air conditioning will be up so high, you can see your breath. And if it's Fall or Winter and it's cold and breezy outside, the theater will have the heat up so high that you will want to be stripped down to your underwear before the opening credits are over. So my mother forgot her wrap, seeing as it was August, and she was cold, she got up out of her seat and went out of the theater and into the attached mall. She hurried into Nordstrom's and picked out a nice sweater, charged it, and made it back to her seat just as the movie was starting. After the movie was over, she walked back to Nordstrom's and politely returned the slightly used sweater.

She bought a dress for a wedding and altered it so it would fit just right. When she saw the wedding pictures, she felt the dress made her look fat. She returned it.

When a clerk asks her the appropriate and proverbial question, "Do you have your receipt?" she just starts to tingle with the opening feelings of the thrill of the game. I am sure there are times when the receipt is hanging out of a pocket of her purse like the tongue of a tired dog, but she will say, "Ah . . . no."

What is the sport if you are within thirty days and have your receipt? The thrill is if you have bought it, worn it, washed it, dried it, dyed it a better color, worn it, altered it, washed it and then returned it! Now that is satisfying.

I wish I could make this a training piece on how everyone can learn to become an expert returner as well, but I cannot. Her skills and talents are unique unto herself. Reminiscent of Mohammad Ali, with his "float like a butterfly, sting like a bee" ploy, she is coy yet relentless. She is the grandmother needing some kindly assistance, yet armed with a rapier wit, able to slice her way through the layers of help until some hapless manager is summoned. At which point they find themselves in front of an endearing, silver, satin-haired lady of grace, looking up at them with innocent, sweet, wide eyes.

"Why, of course, we will take this back. Why did you even have to call me? Give this nice lady her money back."

If one were to pick one return as her finest moment, it would have to be the couch returned to Marshall Field's in Chicago.

She bought an expensive couch from Marshall Field's. We had it for a couple of years, possibly three. It started to lose feathers. This fancy couch was stuffed with goose down. But after a few years, the down, or feathers, started to make their way out onto our living room rug by sneaking between the threads of the linen fabric covering our couch.

The feathers started to show up on a consistent basis, and that began to drive my mother nuts. She called the store and complained. They said the couch was out of warranty, and even if it were still under warranty, the release of a few feathers would not be covered.

The daily feather accumulations continued to increase. My mother drove to Marshall Field's and asked to speak to a manager. She explained the situation and added that if one buys such a supposed, fine product from such a fine store, it shouldn't be leaking feathers all over one's house.

The manager told her he was very sorry, but there was nothing he could do.

"Really?"

My mother drove back home and mused.

Three days later she collected all the feathers that had, let's say, flown the coop, and put them in a plain white envelope. She called the store and asked to speak to the president. Surprisingly, she got him on the phone. She explained that she was a lifelong customer and truly loved his store, but had a problem and wished to make an appointment to speak with him in person. He said that would be fine.

My mother drove back downtown. She went up to the top floor, and after a short wait, was let into the president's office.

"Nice to see you, Mrs. Castle. What seems to be the problem?"

"I bought a couch from you, and it is shedding feathers, and I would like to exchange it for a new one."

"How long ago did you buy this couch?"

"Ah . . . well . . . three . . . ah . . . two years ago."

"I am so sorry Mrs. Castle, but that couch is out of warranty. And even if it were still in warranty, the shedding of a few feathers would most certainly not warrant giving you a new couch."

"Really?"

"Yes. I am so sorry. I wish there was something I could do."

My mother stood up. "I love this store. I have worked in this store. I have shopped here for years. The prices here are not the lowest by any means, but I shop here because I know I will get the finest products and get the very best service." She held up her feather-stuffed white envelope in front of the president's face. "This sir, is three-days' growth from your couch." She then opened the envelope, turned it upside down and shook out the contents, a small, fluttering snowstorm of brown goose feathers, that settled all over the president's desk.

He looked at the feathers, then looked up at her. He pressed the button on his intercom. "Get me furniture. Hello, this is Mr. Walters. I will be sending down a Mrs. Castle in a few minutes. She is to pick out any sofa she wants at no charge. And see to it that it is delivered to her home."

"Thank you so much. Here let me clean these feathers . . ."

"No. No. Just head downstairs and pick out your couch. Thank you for your patronage. And have a very nice day."

So she got a brand new couch with nothing more than an envelope of feathers.

Pretty good.

# The Drive across
# the Country

The second time my mother moved without telling me was a move from Chicago to Seattle. Don't get me wrong, she told me before we actually moved. It's just that she told me after the moving van was near- ly loaded. So after a few days of me hiding at friends' houses and her sitting patiently in a house with no fur- niture, we headed west. Feeling uncharacteristically guilty about uprooting me, she graciously agreed to let my girlfriend Hannah come along on the journey.

We loaded up the big green Pontiac Catalina, picked up Hannah, and got on the road. I have since driven between Chicago and Seattle a number of times, and the length of the trip always varies. I've done it by myself in two and a half days. My friend Doc did it in thirty-six hours once (with the help of medication that, let's just say, is not available over the counter). On this trip though, with my mom at the helm, we scooted across the country in only nine days. Our route, if traced on a map, would very much resemble a cooked piece of spaghetti lying on a kitchen floor. We ate in restaurants for all three meals every day. We would check into a hotel fairly early to relax and enjoy ourselves. Thinking about the actual time we spent driving, it's surprising the three of us are not still somewhere in Montana.

# The Car

How we ended up in the big green Pontiac Catalina is a complete story in itself, which very much exemplifies life with my mother.

We had owned that big green Pontiac Catalina for a long time. It was tired. It was old. It had a turning radius of a three-masted sailing ship. To make a left hand turn, for example, you would have to start spinning the huge wheel frantically to the left, around and around (like Captain Ahab turning the ship to follow the White Whale), about five-hundred feet before the intersection. Then as the large green beast would start to respond as you reached the corner you had to frantically start spinning the wheel the other direction to level it out so as to be able to continue down the road.

This, by the way, was the car I learned to drive in. I remember the first time I drove without an adult in the car. Just Hannah and me. We had just started going out with each other, and here I was, *driving*. Driving her home. I was so nervous. Though it was a beautiful summer day in Chicago, I was terrified. Would I find her house? Would I hit something? What stupid thing might

I do? Well, we made it. No problems. I walked her to the door. Sneaked a little kiss. Went back to the car and heaved a huge sigh of relief. "Phew!" I started up the car, backed out of the driveway and started down the road. And then I saw it. The windshield wipers. Going. Back and forth. The windshield wipers! In August in Chicago on a beautiful sunny day! They had been on the whole time, swish, swish, swish. She had been watching them go for twenty-five minutes. She never made a peep, I'm sure in an effort to not completely embarrass me. Didn't matter. I'm still embarrassed.

My mother decided we needed a new car for the drive across the country. Seeing as I was yet to be let in on the plan that would be moving me away from all my friends on the last day of school before summer break, I just thought buying a new car was a great idea.

My brother Steve has always been a car fanatic. He is a voracious learner and a crafty negotiator. You know that tired expression, "Well, this ain't rocket science?" To Steve, everything is rocket science. So, with Steve armed with more knowledge about automobiles than just about anyone, and to whom dickering with a salesman is a sport, my mother, showing off her version of common sense, went to a dealership . . . by herself.

My mother came home with a new 1973 Mazda. She called Steve to show off her great purchase. I don't know if he started screaming at her all the way over to our house, or waited until he got in front of her, but he was livid. In an effort to keep Steve from popping, she drove to the bank and stopped payment on the check. Then she returned to the dealership and gave the car back.

She then asked, facetiously, "Hey, Steve, would you want to help me buy a new car?" He was, within moments, on it in full-force; cutting out loss leader ads, making phone calls, mapping his strategy. My mother always liked Pontiacs, so my brother found an ad for a brand new Grand Prix. It was listed at a downtown Chicago dealership at a ridiculously low price. Steve, Mom, and I drove there. Steve made us wait in the car while he worked his magic.

He went into the dealership and found the board that listed the sales standings for the month. At the bottom was Mr. Fish. So when they asked Steve if they could help him, he said, "I'm here to see Mr. Fish."

Mr. Fish never had a chance. First, of course, they told Steve the car in the ad was gone, but they had a similar car for only a few thousand dollars more. I don't know how he did it, but after a couple of hours, many trips out to us in the car keeping us updated, many of Mr. Fish's "visits" to the sales manager, Mr. Fish finally sold a car. He ended up selling it at fifty-dollars over what the dealer paid for it. This was later verified by Hannah's father who owned a Cadillac dealership in Chicago until he was extradited out of the county. But, we got it. A beautiful, brand new, olive green Grand Prix with a mahogany dashboard and four miles on the odometer. I was in heaven. I drove that thing around like I was sitting on a throne being carried around by my subjects.

The next day I came back from visiting some friends, eager to get back in my cherished vehicle when . . . when . . . in the driveway . . . there was . . . a different car.

"Hmm." I thought. That's funny. I wonder where the Grand Prix is? What is this blue Le Mans doing in the driveway?

"MOM?"

Seeing as she had only done completely outrageous and unpredictable and unexplainable things, let's say, ah . . . 1000 times before, I started to get nervous.

"MOM?"

"Yes, Cam?"

"Where's the car?"

"Oh, you mean the green one?"

"Ah, huh."

"Oh, I took that back. You see our old car was green. Our couch is green. That new car was green. I am sick of green. I wanted a blue car. So I took that one back. They were very nice. They just traded me straight across. Look, this one has a tinted windshield. The other one didn't. And this car was a Drivers-Ed car; you know what good care they take of those. It only has 12,000 miles on it."

" . . . "

"Cam? Get in. You'll love it!"

" . . . "

"Cam?"

" . . . "

"Cam? You don't like it?"

She agreed to take the blue car back. But the Grand Prix was gone. Gone forever, like the turkey in "A Christmas Story" after the Bumpass's dogs devoured it. Gone.

My mother had a neighbor drive with her in the blue car back to downtown Chicago to the dealership. She had a screwdriver in the car. By a complete miracle, our old car was still parked on the street where she had seen it the day before. She pulled next to it and quickly unscrewed the license plates from the blue car and screwed them back on the old Catalina. She then drove the blue car into the dealership's garage. Got out. Waved to the mechanics. Briskly sauntered out. Jumped into the old car and raced to the bank. The check for the Grand Prix still hadn't cleared, so she stopped payment on it. All was back to the way it was before. Like some bad nightmare concerning a time machine, Mr. Fish still had not technically sold a car. And we were going to drive across the country in the big old green Catalina.

When Steve was somehow able to recompose himself, he graciously agreed to fix up the old car so we might make it. We bought new tires. Loaded up the car. Took with us three eight-track tapes: Leon Russell's "Carney," The Allman Brothers "Live at The Fillmore East," and Johnny Mathis's "Greatest Hits," and headed west.

# The Drive

So, we headed to Seattle. We had the preparation, planning and mapped out strategy reminiscent of Lewis and Clark. No, Magellan. It went like this, "I think I-90 gets us there. We'll just drive 'til we see a Best Western. They're always good. Hey, put in that Johnny Mathis tape. I love him."

And so it went. Our nine-day journey.

As we passed out of the Chicago city limits, we began to get tired and bored.

"I know," said my mom. "Let's go visit my old boy-friend. He owns a clinic in South Dakota. Cam, look at the map. Let's head up there."

Thus was the strategy. Let's drive until an idea pops into someone's head and then point the car in that direction. I later traced our course on a map with magic marker, and it spelled the word "WHY" upside-down and backwards.

We had a fine time meandering around the country. It really was a good way to see more of the country, and it was especially nice to not be in a hurry. My mom had a nice visit with her old boyfriend. We figured he had become a moderate success when we saw that his "clinic" was a massive granite structure with his name carved in five-foot high letters on the outside wall of the top floor. He was very glad to see my mom even though we arrived unannounced after who knows how many years. They reminisced, and Hannah and I opened and put away his rare coin collection that had recently arrived in the mail. I was glad to organize the coins but always wondered how much money someone must have to order an expensive rare coin collection, and then have someone else open it and put it away. Anyway, he gave her a walloping kiss goodbye, and we got back on the road.

Mount Rushmore! Good idea.

With only three eight-tracks, our musical variety was limited. Add to that the fact my mom could not stand the Allman Brothers and could barely tolerate Leon Russell. Hannah and I got real sick of Johnny Mathis. But my mother never got sick of him, and when she would once again sing along "Chances are, when I wear a silly grin . . .", it was always a tad endearing.

We were driving through the Badlands of South Dakota heading for Wyoming, and my mother was asleep in the back. She was sleeping very soundly. So it seemed like a perfect time to . . . smoke some pot. As I mentioned before, back then pot was very different. It was much less potent. It was much more prevalent. And we didn't yet realize how basically stupid it was to get stoned. It was so much less potent then, I think that is why it was called grass. Because many times we smoked stuff that had the same effect as if we were smoking lawn clippings. Who knows, sometimes we probably were. Another thing pot did to my friends and I was stunt our growth in those formative years. Really.

Many years later when my 15 year old son, Mason, 5'10" and aspiring to be a basketball player, asked me, "Dad? Why am I taller than you?" I was quick to tell him about the pot and the growth stunting truth.

Back in the early 70's, you could buy a bag of pot for ten dollars, but before we left Chicago, I purchased a bag of Panama Red. Twenty-five dollars. It was really red. It was. And it was a harbinger of the potent pot that was to come. So, with mom out cold and miles of endless freeway in front of us, we decided to indulge. It was summer, hot out, windows rolled up, the air conditioning on. We brazenly popped in The Allman Brothers and on we drove. Time passed and the scenery wafted by, and an extended guitar duel played on between Duane Allman and Dickey Betts. Hannah and I slowly looked towards each other. And there was my mother. With her chin resting on her folded hands on the top of the bench style front seat of that giant old green Pontiac Catalina. She was smiling. And then she said, in a low undulating tone, *"This music is mellow."*

Hannah and I looked at each other. *My God, my mother is high as a kite and appreciating The Allman Brothers.* She was in an artificially induced euphoric state of nirvana, and she didn't know it. And I was not about to tell her. I was pretty sure my mother had no recollection of The Little Grass Shack episode, and thus, innocent with regards to the enclosed circulating of Panama's finest export. Hannah and I looked at each other with really big eyes and didn't say a word. Slowly my mother slid back to a fetal position, and we drove on quietly, but with our shoulders bobbing up and down continually in silent hysterics.

With my mother still asleep, we drove on and on. I noticed in the distance a beautiful, lush green meadow up on the side of the rolling foothills, very different from the terrain we had been looking at for quite some time. So I pulled over. I was thinking, "Look at that meadow. It doesn't seem that far away. Compared to all the other surroundings, it's quite remarkable. I know. Mom's out like a light. Let's walk up to it. Why not?"

So Hannah and I ran across the interstate, jumped over the guardrail and began our leisurely walk up the small mountain. The meadow was a lot farther away than it looked from the highway. We kept walking. And walking. I was thinking I could hardly wait to finally get there and just roll around on that grass and rest.

"We made it. HUH? This isn't grass."

It was bright green sticker bushes. Little tiny ones. Three inches high. Three inches wide. Two inches apart. Very green, but we not only could not sit down, but if we were to trip and fall down we would've screamed. What the heck?

Hannah and I took a moment to collect ourselves, imbibe in a little more of the Latin American import, and stared off into the horizon. After awhile I remembered my mom and looked down at the car, wondering how she was doing. And that was the first moment we realized what we had done. I had pulled the car over on the interstate, on a curve next to the guardrail that is there to keep vehicles from going over the giant cliff that is a foot from the side of the highway. Semis were whizzing around the curve, barely missing the big old green Pontiac Catalina with my mother asleep in the back. We watched in horror as one after another of those huge trucks careened around the curve. We went "Ahhh!" and took off running back down the mountain, fearing at any second a truck was going to come around that curve thirteen inches farther to the right and send that Catalina, my mother, Leon, Duane and Gregg and Johnny over that cliff.

Back in the car, we drove on, and after a while my mother woke up.

"Have I been asleep long?"

"Nah . . . are you ready to drive?"

"Yeah. I sure am hungry though."

# Mount Rushmore

My mom, Hannah and I followed the signs to the national monument, Mount Rushmore. We were excited. None of us had ever seen it before.

Hannah said, "Look. There's a sign."

"Avoid the crowds. Ride the tram. Get a bird's eye view. Mount Rushmore! The only way to see it!"

Mom pulled in. "It's only seven dollars apiece. A bird's eye view! Let's go."

So we paid our $21.00 and climbed excitedly on the tram.

We rode up, just the three of us on the tram. It was a perfectly lovely afternoon. The view going up was very scenic and serene. As the tram lurched up to the gate at the top of the mount, we excitedly anticipated our experience of witnessing one of our country's finest treasures. We came to a bobbing stop. At the top, to greet us, was a young kid, just sitting in a folding lawn chair reading a book. He looked up at us over his book. The bobbing of the tram gradually stopped, and we were just looking at him through the open window waiting to be released from the car.

"Huh? What are you doin' here?"

"We're here to see Mount Rushmore!" we all said together in a giddily sarcastic way.

"Then why are you here?"

We were still locked in the tram. He was still in his chair.

"What?" asked my mother.

"Why are you here? You can't see the mountain from here. All you need to do is drive another hundred yards or so and you're right at the foot of it. A beautiful view."

Through gritted teeth my mother said, "Could you let us out?"

He finally got up. "Here ya go. Yeah, you can drive right up to it. Not many people come up here."

"Why . . . Do . . . You . . . Sell . . . Tickets . . . Then?" my mother said, trying, yet failing, not to snarl.

"Don't know. I don't sell 'em. Don't know why people would buy 'em."

We stepped out of the tram and with clenched teeth wandered around. It was a lovely place, on a ridge with nice landscaping. There were busts of most of the presidents scattered about.

"Oh, look. There are those pay telescopes. Quick, Mom, give me a quarter."

I put a quarter in the telescope. The lenses clicked open. I focused on a fir tree, then swung the scope to the right, and it slammed to a stop. And there in my view, clear as a bell, was George Washington's right ear. His right ear. That was all. That's as far as the $7.00 plus 25 cent telescope at the "Ride the tram. Beat the crowd," top o' the mount, piece of crap thing would go! His right ear! We were SO pissed.

We got back on the tram. The look we all gave the young kid watching us load ourselves onto the tram should have turned him to salt. We swayed back to ground level, got out, and walked to the ticket booth. My mother demanded our money back. When the ticket taker laughed in her face, my mother composed herself, turned with a smile, and spent the next twenty-five minutes convincing anyone within fifty yards of that booth that if they were to consider giving this woman any money they were idiots and might as well just shoot themselves in the head rather than ride the $21.00 tram to "FUCKING NOWHERE!"

We then got in our car, and as my mother screeched out and to the right, I asked if we could turn around and go left to see Mount Rushmore . . .

Years later, my wife, Laura and I visited Mount Rushmore. You can drive right up to it. It's really cool.

# The Restaurants

On our journey across the country, we ate in a restaurant for nearly every meal. My mother was feeling very flush with the proceeds from selling the house. Today my mother is fiscally responsible. She's generous, but also responsible. It has not always been that way. I was taught, growing up, that if you don't have any money and you don't have any food and no apparent way to get either one right away, what you do is . . . go out to dinner! If you have to be destitute, you might as well enjoy yourself while you're at it. Besides, it will take a while for the check to clear, and by then you might have some money.

The joke I used to tell to describe my mother's lack of frugality goes like this. "The other day, at a tavern near the Glenview Naval Air Station, there were some drunken sailors playing poker, buying drinks for everybody, just throwing money around the bar, when somebody said, 'Hey, you guys are spending money like Dorothy Castle!'"

One night when we were at a very fancy restaurant sitting right next to the piano player, I ordered duck.

Why not? Something different. Duck a l'orange. When it arrived, I took a bite.

"Yuk. It has orange on it. I hate fruit with my meat."

I didn't speak French so how was I supposed to know that orange with an "L" and an apostrophe in front of it was the same as orange in English? It's just the same as the fact that no one knew that was not really Clark Kent, but Superman wearing *glasses*! The piano player leaned over while playing and said, "I'll eat it, kid."

So I put my plate on the piano, and he ate my orangey duck between songs. My mother graciously let me order a hamburger.

One afternoon we were driving in Wyoming, and as we got to a small town, we decided we'd had enough driving for that hour, so we looked for a motel. After we checked in and relaxed for a while, we headed out to find a restaurant. This was a very small town. There didn't seem to be any restaurants. That's impossible. We saw a tavern, and my mother opened the door and popped her head in. There was no one in there but a bartender.

My mom asked, "Do you serve food?"

"Yup."

"Can they come in?" she asked, pointing to her teenage companions, Hannah and me.

"Yup."

We all walked in past the creaky door and sat at the bar. It was dark inside, even though it was sunny outside. The bar seemed very old, the wood polished from many years of rubbing from elbows or hands. It was a narrow room with just one row of tables against the wall behind us.

My mother asked, "Do you have a menu?"

"Nope."

"Hmm."

"Three dinners?" he asked.

We said, "Yup."

The bartender opened up a refrigerated drawer and pulled out three New York steaks. He tossed them into a small, home model, electric fry pan, and they started to sizzle. When they were done, he flopped them on a plate, opened a heated drawer, and pulled out three baked potatoes. He squeezed them, dolloped on some butter, and slid the plates in front of us. We each looked at each other, picked up our knife and fork, cut a bite of steak and put it in our mouths. We looked at each other again.

With mouths full, all three of us mumbled at the same time, "This is the best bite of food I have ever had in my life!"

The bartender folded his arms across his chest, leaned back against the back bar, and just beamed a great big "I knew that" smile.

The next morning my mother came into my room and woke me up. She had been having a hard time getting teenagers "up and at 'em" in the morning. Sometimes we wouldn't get on the road until 10:00 A.M. Couple that with stopping for lunch at noon, and it didn't make for covering much ground.

That morning she came in and said, "Its nine o'clock. Let's go. You promised today we could get an earlier start."

I got out of bed, splashed water on my face and brushed my teeth. Hannah and Mom were packed and ready to go. I crawled into the car. My mom backed out of the parking space and pulled out onto the street. Then I looked at the clock.

"Six o'clock! What the heck?"

With both hands on the huge steering wheel of the big green Pontiac Catalina, leaning forward with enthusiastic determination, as we were heading swiftly down the side street behind the motel, she confessed, "I had to lie to you. It was the only way to get you in this car early."

Just then we pulled up to the intersection of Main Street, the highway we needed to take out of town. And at that moment my mother's clever plan evaporated, because, sauntering down Main Street at 6:00 A.M. that morning were approximately 2,000 head of cattle. At that moment two things became very clear. We were not going to get an early start, and we now understood why that dinner was *so* good.


Next stop Boise, Idaho, to visit my dad.
But first . . .

# A Word about My Father

So far, I've written very little about my father, an amazing man who deserves his own book. But until then, here is a bit about him and the remarkable contrast between my parents. Complete polar opposites. I used to describe how different they were in this way:

If, for example, my father was in a grocery store and wanted to find which shelf the mayonnaise was on, he would walk attentively down each aisle. Even if he passed an employee stocking the shelves, he wouldn't bother him because he wouldn't want the person to have to stop what they were doing and trudge around the store, pointing out something my father could figure out on his own.

My mother, upon realizing she needed mayonnaise and that she didn't know where it was, would stop in her tracks and shout, "Anybody know where the mayonnaise is?"

Or, on a bad day, would yell, "Whose stupid idea was it to hide the mayonnaise?"

# A Brief History of
# My Father

**M**y sister Kim and I went to see our father in the hospital after he had his second major cancer surgery. The nurse said we could go in to his room, that he was doing fine.

"He's very funny," she said.

Kim and I looked at each other like, "When did he have a chance during surgery to be funny?"

When we went into his room, what we saw shocked us. He was white, with tubes coming out of him from all over the place. He looked dead. We quickly turned to go out of the room. The nurse was behind us. She said, "Go on," and gestured for us to go to him.

We walked up to his bed and he noticed us. He started mumbling something, but the tubes in his mouth and throat made it hard for us to understand. He kept repeating it very determinedly. We finally made it out, "Pencil, paper. Pencil, paper."

"Oh, my. He wants to write his will!" we thought.

I gave him paper and pencil and he quickly jotted this down:

At five o'clock it's time to drink

No need for icy cubes

Nor glasses for the booze I think

Just pour it down the tubes

He had thought up this limerick during recovery and was afraid he would forget it. That was our dad. Strength through adversity with humor.

When Dad went in for the fateful MRI that would find the cancer in his mouth again, there was something he hadn't told us. As they were leading him into the big magnet room, they asked, "Oh, by the way, are you claustrophobic?"

"Yes, very," he answered in a quite bothered manner. Uh, oh.

Kim and I said, "We didn't know that. You never told us."

"I've always been."

One year, at our family summer cottage in Northport, Michigan, I was on my way out of the cabin to play golf with Uncle Bruce.

As I grabbed my clubs that were leaning under the bookcase, Bruce said to me, "Your dad is in that book."

I looked up, and he was pointing at *Heroes of World War II.*

I looked over at my father and asked, "You are?"

"Ah . . . yeah."

"Why didn't you ever tell me?"

"You never asked."

So Kim and I were not surprised to find out, about three or four decades late, that he was claustrophobic. But we realized we had a problem. The MRI consisted of the subject being slid into a large white tube that is a giant magnet and staying completely still for an hour. He was terrified and felt he just couldn't do it. At one point he couldn't take it, and they pulled him out for a couple minutes. They talked to him, put Glenn Miller on headphones, and he agreed to try it again.

He made it. He was in there over an hour. He hated it. And this is what he said when it was over,

There once was an old man from Boise
Who got in trouble for being too noisy
So they stuffed him in a tube
The silly old boob
And shot him off to New Joisy

He said he couldn't come up with anything else to rhyme with Boise – it kept him occupied.

The combination in one man of such strength and bravery with such kindness and wit, coupled with an unending desire to never bother, or put anybody out, made him truly the most remarkable person I've ever known.

Every person who ever came into contact with him left a little better off because of it. Whether it was the waitress at the Copper Kettle restaurant or the owner of Albertson's, he treated them the same; as friends. He liked people, and wanted people to like him. And they did.

The real test would have been if he had ever met Rush Limbaugh. But if he were forced to spend some time with him, he would have come up with something positive to say about him.

It was during one of his tirades about Rush Limbaugh when I was visiting in Boise, that he choked on a piece of steak.

After his second surgery (the first being a lung removal), he was told he would never eat solid food again. He loved food. He loved to cook. He even compiled a cookbook from his favorite recipes. He was determined to eat solid food again. I think it was a scone at the Puyallup Fair that did it. He managed to get that down, and after that, with much determination and work, he eventually made it to eating anything, including a filet mignon, which he would have handled fine if we hadn't gotten on the topic of Rush.

So, at the emergency room, Dad was in a room and doing fine. The doctor came in and sat down next to him. "How are you?"

"Fine."

"Yes, you are . . . fine." The doctor got up and left.

A few minutes later he came back in, sat down, and scooted his chair closer.

"So . . . how are you?"

"Fine."

"Yes, you are." The doctor got up and left again.

Dad and I looked at each other. A few moments later, the doctor came in *again*.

"So, Bob, you're doing fine." He said it more like a question than a statement.

"Yup."

"Fine," repeated the doctor.

"Yup."

"Really? No problem?"

"No."

"Ok, I guess you can go."

So we got ready and went out into the hall. As we passed the nurses' station, we saw four doctors looking at an x-ray and laughing.

"Dad, they're laughing at your x-ray."

They all go, "No, no, we're . . ."

Dad said, "It's ok. You can laugh at my x-ray."

With a sheepish look, ducking his head in his shoulders, the doctor said, "Yes. We are laughing at your x-ray. I called in these specialists. We, uh . . . we couldn't . . . uh . . . we've never seen anything like it. Uh . . . we're not sure why . . . you're . . ."

"Alive?" my dad cheerfully offered.

"Yes! Ah . . . ah . . ."

"I had a lung removed."

The doctor slapped his forehead, and all of the other doctors let out a big sigh. "OH!!!"

"I guess I should have mentioned that."

(Hmm . . . familiar theme.)

"We've never seen an x-ray like that before. How long ago did you have the operation?" asked the doctor.

"Fifteen years ago."

Silence.

The doctor said, "Wow. Well . . . have a good day Mr. Castle. It was a pleasure to meet you."

\* \* \*

After the divorce my father moved into an apartment in downtown Chicago. It was a huge building. I think he lived on the 35th floor. It was not a very happy place. I know my dad missed the comfy house and big yard.

He used to spend hours on the weekends in the summer sitting cross-legged on the front lawn of our house, pulling crab grass, unwinding from the incredibly stressful job of owning and running a company he didn't want to own. The company was the Chicago Flag and Decorating Company that he took over after his father passed away. The biggest customer, by the way, was Wrigley Field, where, at that time, the Bears and the Cubs both played. I often got to enjoy the benefits of that. But, a divorce, the job he didn't want, and the small apartment 35 floors higher than he wanted to be, all added together to be very tough on him.

I was eight years old when he lived in that apartment. I remember he had a small rectangular dish, maybe four by six inches, which had grass growing in it. Though he cut it with scissors, he had a miniature lawn mower parked on it.

I spent a lot of time looking out the window at the city. It was fascinating to be that high up. There always was a dish of Jordan Almonds on the window sill. Those are almonds with a hard, colored candy coating. I have no idea why he always had them because I never saw him eat one. But he replenished them, and I was glad because, when he wasn't looking, I would open the window and throw them, one at a time. I was amazed at how far away from the building they would travel. Just giving one a slight arc, magnified over 350 feet, or so, that almond would make it past the parking lot and to the street. I threw a lot of them. Never all, or he might think something was up, but I threw a lot of them. It was lucky I didn't kill somebody.

The furniture was awful. Faded, yellow-orange corduroy. He smoked two packs of unfiltered Lucky Strikes a day, so the place was dingy. All that added up to an extra hard situation because my dad's default emotions were happy and funny. Though he didn't want to move away from his little son, the decision to move to Boise, Idaho, saved him. He was stationed in Boise before and after his active duty in the war. He had some close friends there and moving there was perfect for him.

One of his most remarkable stories about moving to Boise had to do with The Arid Club. The Arid Club has always been the most exclusive in Boise.

I can hear Joan Rivers now saying, "So what?" When I used to call on Boise as part of my three state territory, a factory contact I often called for assistance retold her joke to me most times I called in. It goes like this. "You know the only thing worse than having your plane crash? Having it land safely in Boise, Idaho." Funny joke, but ridiculous because Boise is a great town that has an amazing wealth of excellent restaurants.

During the war, since my father was an officer, he was given membership into the club. Twenty-five years later, after moving back, he was invited to the club with a member. When the maître d opened the large wooden doors and saw my father, he said, "Good evening, Captain Castle. Nice to see you again. Would you like to follow me? Could I get you a bourbon and water?"

My father could not believe it. Twenty-five years later the guy not only remembered his name and rank, but his favorite drink.

After living in Boise for a few years, he bought a condo on the golf course of Hillcrest Country Club. When I visited, I would get to play golf with him on that fabulous golf course. One afternoon I hit yet another terrible drive. This one landed near the fence by the road on some neglected patch of dirt. The course was gorgeous, but my shot was so awful that my ball was in an area the groundskeeper need not worry about. The lie was nearly unhittable. Closer to the fairway I saw some big chalk circles drawn on the ground. I asked my dad what those were.

"Ground under repair. If you had landed inside one of those circles, you could move your ball."

"Darn. Who decides what is ground under repair?"

"The grounds committee. Wait. I forgot. I'm the president of the grounds committee. I deem this ground under repair. You may move your ball."

It's not what you know . . .

# The Drive Continues
# to Boise

**M**om pulled the Catalina off I-84 onto the second exit, following the sign to the Travelodge. A right hand turn and a couple of blocks presented to us our familiar, and to my mother, comforting, Sleepy Bear logo. That bear, wearing his nightcap, and walking with his arms out-stretched, conveyed to my mom "ah, serenity." To Hannah and me, it evoked, "I hate that stupid bear. How is it peaceful thinking he might just sleep-walk into our room some night? These motels smell like cheap air fresheners and don't have restaurants!" But that bear logo made my mom so content that we never inkled out a molecule of ridicule so as to diminish her enthusiasm.

Thinking back, I don't remember any nervous or awkward feelings about coalescing my parents together again. There was a big party planned for that afternoon with the teeming group of my father's close friends. He had many friends: bowling teams, golfing buddies, bridge playing foursomes, college football tailgating enthusiasts, but most of all, cocktail party throwing, fun-loving pals.

My dad was so happy there. He had been living in Boise for about six years at that time and had a lady friend that he had been quite quiet about. I remember at the party wondering which lady it was. They got married soon after, and as I mentioned earlier, my mother and father were so comfortable with the divorce and the other's spouse, that some years later they planned to all go on a trip together.

After resting up in our motel rooms, Mom, Hannah, and I headed out to try to find the house of my dad's best friend who was hosting the party. Boise is not an easy town to navigate through. Years later it was part of my sales territory, and I remember getting surprisingly lost trying to get between two spots that were not very far from each other. It almost seems like, instead of grids, the street layout is like the spokes of two wheels lying next to each other.

After a lot of muttering by my mother, and lots of useless suggestions by me, we somehow found the house. The ride was less painful than it could have been because the radio stations Hannah and I were flipping through were great. We had spent days going through "Country" country, but here the music was as hip as it could get, and all over the dial. Later we realized we were in a college town, and the radio stations catered to, or were run by, the large percentage of college age kids.

When we walked in the house, we were all knocked back just a bit by the profoundly joyous atmosphere. There were about thirty folks laughing and mingling, munching food, smoking cigarettes, and clinking ice cubes in frosty cocktail glasses. They were all expecting us and glad to greet us, but it was obvious that this party wasn't because of us; it was a very regular event that coincided with our visit. These people were happy.

My dad was a bit nervous to start, but loved meeting Hannah. He was glad to see me, of course, but it was mildly painful for him to accept my long hair. It was light brown, wavy, and to the middle of my back. Sports were always a big part of my relationship with my dad. Seeing me gain four yards in the freshman high school football game was a giant highlight in his life as a father. So the fact that from the back I looked like the sultry model in the Breck shampoo ads, made him a bit squirmy.

We chatted and mingled and finally were introduced to a quiet lady with freshly saloned, full brown hair. She had been sitting in a chair in a far corner ever since we had entered. She was not introduced as Bob's girlfriend, but as just Mackie. Her uncomfortableness made it obvious. So my mother took over, grabbing her hand and diving into stories about our trip. If my mother ever sees someone who is uncomfortable in any way, she will immediately try to diagnose and solve the problem. As long as it is a quick fix. She is like AAA as opposed to AA. If you need a tow, she is right there. If you need long term compassion, "I don't have time for that."

It was quite a raucous and friendly party, with drinks flowing. It also was 3:00 in the afternoon on a pretty sunny day. Hannah and I would look at each other and telepathically share the thought that this is how we hoped college would be, not imagining that it was also possible for retired folks. Cool.

At one point a big fellow in his early twenties, came through the door. Anyone in the room who noticed, stopped what they were doing and remarked, or waved, or "Oohed."

My dad's best friend shouted, "Hey, Ron. Glad you could make it. Say hi to Bob's ex-wife Dodo, and her son Cam. And his girlfriend. That's Ron, my son."

I shook his hand. He was strong and beaming with confidence. Nice looking guy, dressed sharp in pressed slacks and a logoed sweater. He moved on, and the person closest to me beat some others in telling me who Ron was. "He's on the Boise State football team. One of their star players. He should make All-American. Offensive tackle. He is amazing."

Ron was loving the attention and soaking up the adoration. Not annoyingly cocky, just proud of himself, and it seemed it was probably well deserved. He was fielding all sorts of questions and not holding back with his answers. The topic came up of arm wrestling. I am not exactly sure why. But what came next I'll never forget. The dynamic of the room changed from random mingling to a small arena setting with Ron in the middle. At the back of the circled crowd was a thin, fifty or sixty year old man. Scrawny really. He had been sitting in a chair, unimpressed, while the rest of the group crowded around the football star. Holding an amber colored drink with tinkling ice cubes, the thin, elderly man stood up and said, "Arm wrestling. I used to be very good at it."

He was ignored, and Ron returned to bragging about how he had beaten everyone on his team.

"Really, it is not strength that is important. It is all timing and leverage." said the man.

No one seemed to hear him. I was standing next to him and something about the guy intrigued me. He exuded a quiet confidence that was palpable. Not like the boisterous star.

"I can beat you."

Finally people stopped cooing over Ron and looked at the man.

"What?" Ron asked with a look, that said, don't interrupt me, I'm in the middle of a story here. Go back to your bourbon and water.

"Yes. I can beat you."

"Don't be ridiculous."

"I bet you a hundred dollars I can beat you."

"I don't want your money. And I would be afraid I might break your arm."

The man reached in his back pocket, pulled out his wallet, and took out a hundred dollar bill. He walked over and slapped it on the coffee table. At this point, Ron seemed to realize that he was going a bit overboard with his bravado and had nothing against this friend of his dad's.

"Please pick up your money. I don't want to do this. You could really get hurt."

The man took a big swig from his drink, set it down, and rolled up his right sleeve. "I've arm wrestled my whole life. As I said, it's all timing and leverage, not strength." He knelt down on the floor and placed his elbow on the table. Everyone backed up a little.

Ron said, "I don't want your money. Fine. We can go once. I'll be careful. But put your money away."

"Okay." The man put his bill back in his wallet and knelt back down.

Ron let out a big sigh, pushed the sleeve of his sweater past his elbow and knelt down. They clasped hands and fidgeted.

No one could believe it had gotten this far. Ron was easily over 250 pounds of muscle. The older man couldn't have weighed more than 120 pounds. He was pale with a yellowish hue from all the cigarette smoke. He looked like the only solid stuff he ate was an occasional ice cube from his drink.

"Ready?" said the man.

"Any time."

And "wham." The man slammed Ron's wrist back onto the table with a loud thud.

Everyone gasped, including Ron, who then caught himself, cleared his throat and slightly bewildered, said, "Sorry. I must not have been ready. Let's go again."

"No problem," said the man.

Ron shook his shoulders, took in a deep breath and positioned his elbow again. They clasped hands. Ron tensed every muscle in his body.

The man said, "Ready?"

"Yup."

Wham! Ron's wrist and forearm hit the table with a loud slap.

Everyone in the room was blown away.

They all started muttering. "How did he do that? Ron, you're letting him win. How is that possible? Well, I have never seen anything like that."

They tried it a number of more times, and the man always won. Ron finally gave up. And rather than be embarrassed or angry, Ron just looked at the old man with deep admiration, stood up and shook his hand. "That was amazing. Can you teach me about that?" And they went over to the wet bar, and the old man poured two big drinks. Both of which he drank.

They served an early and delicious dinner. We said our goodbyes and thank you's, and left for our motel. As we left, it felt like, rather than winding down, that party was just revving up.

For the first time on the trip, we went to bed early because the final leg of this trip to Seattle would be a long one.

So we left Boise, Idaho, leaving behind my father and his friends, and the fabulous radio stations. We headed toward Seattle, troubadoured by our three 8-track tapes.

"Chances are, cause I wear a silly grin . . ."

# Seattle

Nine days after we headed west, we pulled the Catalina into my brother Truman's driveway in Bellevue, Washington. Compared to the pioneers and their covered wagons, we might have well been in a rocket. But compared to travelers making the same trip since, oh, let's say, 1940, we might have well been on bicycles.

Included in the lack of planning on our zigzag across the country was, "Where the hell are we going to live once we get there?"

There is nothing more typical in thinking about my mother than finding oneself in a situation like this.

Sell the house. Order the moving van. Pack up everything. Buy a new car. Return a new car. Buy a new car. Trade it for a used car. Return used car. Retrieve old car. Buy new tires. Drive a few thousand miles. Pull into a driveway.

"Made it. Now what?"

She decided to move to Seattle, sold the house and moved, and actually never gave a thought as to where we were going to live.

How my mother chose Seattle is a story in itself.

Truman graduated from law school at Duke University, got married, and somehow ended up in Toledo, Ohio. Not meaning to demean Toledo in general, I can only speak of the part of the neighborhood Truman and his young bride lived in. When my mother and I came to visit them, I being thirteen or so, I will never forget sitting at their metal dinette dining room set and playing gin rummy. I remember it vividly for two reasons. First, one hand I was dealt was a ten card run of hearts, which I have never come close to duplicating. And, second, out their kitchen window, directly in one's field of vision, down the street that ended in a T, was the billboard for the continuous show of the big star, Alexandra The Great 48!

My teenage hormones were just starting to consider causing a ruckus, and there, as I was playing gin rummy with my mother, I was staring at a humongous billboard that advertised the giant chest of Toledo's biggest star.

In the billboard picture, she was blond and lovely. And each breast, I figured if I were to leave my metal chair and walk down the street to measure, was easily the size of a Volkswagen. I also, though young, was mildly wise enough to suspect the painted rendition was a tad old, and Ms. Alexandra looked nothing like the advertisement. I didn't care. I was very curious.

My brother and his wife were ready to get out of Toledo and move west. They decided on Denver. Then some very good friends came to visit one week before Truman was picking up the U-Haul trailer. They showed a slide show of Seattle and talked it up so much that

Truman and Candy changed their minds and decided to aim the car a little farther north and west.

A few years later, my sister graduated from Michigan State and got married. Her husband, Bruce, said, "I will get a job anywhere you want to live. Where shall it be?"

She said, "Seattle, to be near my brother."

That brings us back to Truman's driveway. My sister Kim and her husband Bruce were there, standing in the driveway, to greet us when we pulled up. Hugs and "whoops" all around, then into the house. We had been in Seattle, Bellevue actually, for over a minute and already a family party.

We were sitting around the living room, chatting and chuckling. Mom was rattling off highlights of our drive. Hannah and I were having to hold back from sharing our favorite memories that included getting Mom stoned while she slept and leaving her in the parked car on the treacherous curve on the mountain road as we pranced up the hill to smoke more pot.

Eventually, someone brought up the question of where my mother and I planned to live.

"Hmm. That's funny, that thought never crossed my mind. Gosh, Cam, I was so busy with selling and packing and moving and driving, thinking about where to live just slipped my mind. But, I don't know, things just always sort of work themselves out."

"You know," offered Candy, "we are selling this house. We were just about to put it on the market. Would like to buy this one?"

"I'd love to!" said my mom, getting that glint in her eye and rubbing her hands together.

"Truman, what do you think? Do you want to sell this to your mother?"

"Hmm, well . . . let's see. I was . . . well, thinking, hmm. That might be a . . ." replied Truman in his lawyerly fashion we have come to expect and love through the years.

"How much were you thinking of asking?" said my mom with the tone one would have while reaching for their checkbook.

Truman said a number like $35,000 or something, that looking back, sounds so ridiculously small.

Candy chimed in, "Oh, Truman, it's your mother. That is way too much."

Then Truman, making a face similar to one appearing on the face of a prostate exam recipient, knocked a couple thousand off the previous reasonable price.

"Sold!" announced my mother. Clinking of glasses all around, and she and I got to move into Truman's fabulous house with the view of Lake Washington, the Space Needle and Mount Rainier.

Until she sold it without telling me a few years later.

# My Mother in an Emergency

It was a miracle that we got to move into my brother's house. The sub-division was called Cherry Crest because it was filled with cherry trees that, when in bloom, were awe-inspiring. I made close friends with kids my age who lived within throwing distance of our house. My senior year was a breeze because, when they transferred my grades from one of the top schools in the country, New Trier, I had enough credits to graduate before I started my senior year at the school in Bellevue. I was, though, missing the requirement of one semester of Washington State History, which surprisingly wasn't offered at New Trier in Illinois. I added in six electives to my class schedule and graduated a half a year early.

We chose that time to have my wisdom teeth removed. Four of them.

I was on our comfy, green velour couch in the den. In a dopey, narcotic pain-killer induced dream state, I was listening to Neil Young's "Time Fades Away," a live recording that was soothing to my Darvocet adjusted ears. Though if today I were to review Neil's decades-spanning diverse and prolific catalogue, "Time Fades Away" is really quite a discordant, loud, haphazard collection, which could sound to many like a recording of the recycling truck making its pre-dawn neighborhood pick up.

To me it was soothing. So soothing in fact that as I lay there propped up and pleasant, I was oblivious to the fact that I had earlier agreed to make lunch for my mother and me.

We were going to have tacos. I had browned the meat and chopped the lettuce and tomatoes. I had grated the cheese. I had put the oil in the large fry pan on the stove. Turned it to "high."

"Man, I love this song. He can play guitar *and* harmonica *at the same time*! Wow.

That's a funny smell. Hmm. What am I forgetting? THE OIL! AHHH!"

I leapt from the couch. My narcotic induced ocean cruise with Mr. Young was immediately washed away. In the kitchen on the stove was the 10" fry pan with a perfectly symmetrical 10" wide cylinder of white smoke reaching to the ceiling.

I possess a peculiar trait that is either an attribute or a fault depending on who you are talking to. In a crisis I become very calm. I am sure that is because in a crisis my mother becomes incredibly . . . ah . . . uncalm. All my life, whether it's a catastrophe such as abruptly stopping the car so as to make the covered pan containing the still warm pot roast dinner hurtle forward and land open and upside down on the floor of the car, or merely being late in leaving for a family party, her reaction is always the same. Screaming.

So, I always remain calm. Today, my young son interprets my reaction to mean I don't care about him and his banged shin. My mother always interprets it as me not having a clue as to what is happening. "WE ARE LATE! CAN'T YOU GET THAT THROUGH YOUR HEAD?"

I was in the kitchen, looking at this perfectly shaped plume of smoke, and in a loud yet composed voice said to my mother, who was down the hall, in her bed, reading her book, "Mom. We have a problem."

She was out of her bed, down the hall and in the kitchen in a flash. Some positives associated with the over-reactive package are cat-like reflexes and instantaneous responses, usually accompanied with screaming.

I looked past the plume and saw the exhaust fan for the kitchen. This particular setup was a round hole in the kitchen wall open to the backyard. Little louvered shutters keep the opening covered. Attached to that was a small fan. You'd pull on a chain and the shutters would pop open, then you flick the switch on the fan.

I reached past the plume that was still in full billow and tugged on the chain and released it. The shutters popped open, and before I could flick the switch on the fan, a glorious scientific demonstration about the elements needed to create the amazing physical phenomenon called fire, were vividly presented to my mother and me. One needs a flammable material, heat and... OXYGEN!

Opening the little porthole supplied plenty of the stuff. The pan burst into flames. It was a 10" wide round cylinder of fire reaching two feet in the air. "Oh my God!" we both yelled.

My mother and I looked at each other, and again in unison said, "Salt!"

She said, "I can't remember, you either pour salt on an oil fire or you don't."

"I can't remember either. I'll try it."

The salt ignited like a miniature fireworks display, each granule bursting into a colorful round flame, many igniting, it seemed, before they even reached the fire.

"Salt bad," I said.

I thought to myself, "*Dirt!*" So I headed to the back door off the dining room to grab some dirt from the flowerbeds. As I passed through the dining room, I saw in the corner, the cat box. Besides being calm in a crisis, I also possess the very annoying habit of trying to interject humor. As I passed the cat box, I said, (jokingly) "I know, kitty litter!" then hurried out the door.

I was back in two seconds. But in those two seconds, like people who can lift cars off of loved ones, my over-reacting and suddenly athletically gifted mother had managed to sprint out, grab the cat box and pour its contents onto the fire.

Now, if any of you are imagining a box of clean ecru-colored particles of clay that, wondrously, cats are drawn to relieve themselves in, and that those clay-like substances would likely be a fine material to pour onto an oil fire, you would be wrong.

That would be because this cat box was not filled with your traditional clay-like kitty litter. No. It contained "Litter- Green." Old "Litter-Green." Very old and needing to be changed "Litter-Green."

And, for those of you who might not be familiar with the product, let me fill you in. It is not clay. It is not a natural substance whatsoever. It is green polypropylene, chlorophyll infused pellets. Pellets infused now, thanks to our lovely cat Angel, with much nastier ingredients than mere chlorophyll.

Guess what else? It burns. It burns really well, giving off a toxic gas that the inventers and marketers of this odd product never tested for, most likely because they were probably unable to come up with a scenario where it might become a problem. "Hey Bob, what if this stuff catches on fire?"

"What are you talking about Al? Why would anyone set kitty litter on fire? Forget about it."

They didn't grow up anywhere near my mother.

Staring at my mother in complete disbelief, I tossed my two handfuls of dirt on the fire which immediately extinguished it, save for the bubbling and undulating mass of molten, urine infused, polypropylene, formerly chlorophyll flavored, "Litter-Green" pellets.

With the fire out, we were now able to have a conversation. I went first.

"WHY DID YOU DO THAT?"

"YOU TOLD ME TO!"

"I WAS KIDDING!"

"WHY WOULD YOU KID IN A CRISIS? THAT IS JUST PLAIN STUPID!"

"NO. POURING STINKING KITTY LITTER ON A FIRE IS STUPID!"

We swiftly moved our shouting match out of the kitchen because the toxic fumes were so intense they were making our eyes and throats burn. In the living room, we couldn't even see the picture window, the smoke was so thick.

"I CAN'T BELIEVE YOU . . ."

"I CAN'T BELIEVE *YOU* . . ."

We had to repaint the kitchen, dining room and the living room.

My mother got over her anger at me for my idiotic trait of trying to crack a joke in a crisis. And secretly . . . just loved the chance to pick out all new paint colors for those three rooms.

# A Realization

I have compared my mother to I Love Lucy and to Peter Pan, but recently I have had a realization.

My mother is also a cross between Katherine Hepburn and George Costanza's father.

Katherine Hepburn possessed the perfect melding of natural elegance without a shred of pretension.

On the show Seinfeld, George Costanza's father only said things he believed very strongly to be true, but said them very loudly.

Blend those two dichotomous characters into one person, and you have my mother.

"Why, these cucumber sandwiches are wonderful. Is this Hollywood bread? That is my favorite. Cam? Why aren't you eating your sandwich?"

"It's stupid. It's just pickles that don't taste like anything on this small dry bread. I hate it. Can I have something else? Can I have peanut butter and jelly instead? And why didn't you buy me that jawbreaker? I wanted that. I want a jaw breaker."

"Please eat the sandwich Grandma Bessie made for you. It is very nice. I love it. And no, YOU CANNOT HAVE A PEANUT BUTTER AND JELLY SANDWICH! AND IF YOU MENTION THAT JAW BREAKER AGAIN... YOU KNOW WHAT I WILL DO? I WILL GO AHEAD AND BREAK YOUR JAW. AND I MEAN IT! HOW DO YOU FEEL ABOUT THAT? Bessie the soup is very nice also. Is it leek? Subtle and very good. Now Cam, put your napkin in your lap."

My childhood was the omnipresent entwining of,

"Oh, doesn't he look nice?"

And,

"SERENITY NOW! SERENITY NOW!"

It's a wonder I can dress myself.

# My Son is Better than Your Son

How I wish my mother had talked that way. Instead, what I got was, "Why can't you be more like . . .?"

All mothers think their children are the best, and many mothers make a point of telling anyone who will listen that that is the case.

"My son is on the honor roll."

"My son made the varsity basketball team."

"My son hasn't been arrested once this year."

Moms are always bragging about their kids. That is, except mine. She felt the most important attributes she could try to help me to attain were humility and a desire to excel. Thus, to positively reinforce me at any time would be counter-productive to both those goals.

After my mother and I moved to Bellevue, Washington, I got a job in a restaurant for five dollars an hour. It was just Mom and I living in a condo. I came home one day after a long shift, and she said, "I just got off the phone with your Aunt Elva. You know her son Andy, your cousin? Well, she told me that he works in a restaurant just like you, in Chicago, only he doesn't just work there. No. He is the manager. He makes five hundred dollars a week, and you know what else? He is best friends with ah . . . the Cubs shortstop. Don something."

"Don Kessinger? He's best friends with Don Kessinger?"

"Yes. Best friends. He comes in all the time. Andy's the manager, you know. Making five hundred dollars a week. He runs the place. What do you do? You should be more like your cousin. I can't believe you are just some, whatever you do at that restaurant, when you could be running the place like your cousin Andy. You just don't have any gumption. You need to be more assertive."

I felt like crap. My cousin, who was almost exactly my age, was Mr. Restaurant superstar back in Chicago, palling around with one of my favorite Cubs. And what was I doing? Prepping food in the kitchen of "The Great American Disaster" restaurant. As I was slopping canned refried beans onto forty dry tortillas, before wrapping them in plastic wrap and tossing them in the walk-in, my cousin was cashing his big paycheck and heading off to box seats at Wrigley Field.

Later that summer I took the train to Chicago to visit all my friends. With no real plan, I just stayed at different friends' houses and had a wonderful, carefree time. One night my friend Brett had a big barbeque. His parents were very well off, living in an affluent part of the North Shore of Chicago. They had a huge house with a built-in swimming pool. As I was milling around the party that had at least a hundred people, I bumped into my cousin Andy.

"Andy! How the heck are you? I didn't know you knew Brett."

"Oh, yeah. Everybody knows Brett. When did you get into town?"

"Just a few days ago. Man, it's nice to see you. I sure have heard a lot about you. I am so impressed. Damn, I am so envious. My mother told me all about your job and everything."

"Huh?"

"Yeah. Your job. Making all that money. Being the manager. And being best friends with Don Kessinger. Shit, I'm just a prep cook. I can't believe how much you make."

"What the hell are you talking about? I'm a prep cook at Henry's. I make five dollars an hour. Don Kessinger? He came in once and I said "hi" to him. But my mother told me that you were managing a restaurant in Seattle and were making who knows how much money. I felt like crap. She kept saying, 'Why can't you be more like your cousin Cam.' You mean to tell me they were both lying to us?"

At that moment Andy and I were quiet, and I felt we were both doing the same thing; starting to reflect on the possible magnitude of the realization that our mothers would use, in an effort to motivate us, complete fabrications, or in my mother's case an occasionally dysfunctional memory. I could sense that Andy, like me, was also starting a quick inventory of all the possible whoppers told in order for us to be prodded in a desired direction. It was a significant moment in both our lives, and I remember exactly what he said next.

"Do you want another beer, Cam?"

"Yup."

# Threats

Most parents have their own unique stable of threats and warnings that they use to influence their children's behavior. There is the old, "You'll poke your eye out." Or, "You're going to break your neck." My ex-mother-in-law was very creative with her threats. "Stop doing that or I will tear your arm off and beat you with it."

I had my own ridiculous threat to my kids. "You're slap happy. Do you know what that means? That means we get to slap you until we're happy." I never did of course, but simply saying that little turn of a phrase would get them to think just long enough to lose interest in whatever annoying activity they were engaged in.

My trouble was that my mother, as with most aspects of her mothering, was the opposite of other moms. Instead of, "Don't run with scissors." My mother would say, "Bring me the scissors. No. The pointy ones. And hurry!"

When she had just had it with me, she would consistently suggest, "Why don't you go outside and play on the freeway?"

Thinking back on it, I was a horribly annoying son. The problem was that she taught me to never take "no" for an answer, to stand up for what I wanted, and to be aggressive. What she didn't realize was that she was the focus of most of my requests and needs. So, if I asked if I could be driven to Mike's house at nine-o'clock at night to spend the night, her simple "no" would have no effect. I remember lying on the kitchen floor re-asking her repeatedly, incessantly, to be driven to Mike's house.

"No," she would say over and over. And I would keep asking. At one point she was so mad at my constant barrage, she turned from doing the dishes and fired a metal spatula at me so hard the corner of it stuck in the linoleum. I slid back out of the kitchen, sat on the dining room carpet and said, "Please???" Why give up? She didn't hit me with the spatula, and whether she had or not, I really wanted to go to Mike's house.

After my second, "Please???" from the dining room, she got eerily quiet. She turned again, dried her hands and said, slowly and softly, "Fine. Let's go."

I was thrilled. It worked. She taught me well. We got in the '65 yellow Mustang and backed out of the driveway. She headed down our street, the serene, tree-lined Arbor Lane, her hands gripping the wheel so tight I thought it might crumble to dust. She started driving faster. Then she turned to me, and with eyes glazed over and a sardonic smile on her face said, "I am going to drive this car into a tree." She was going about 60 miles per hour down our quiet street. "I am so mad at you I would rather kill us both than drive you to your friend's house." Then she yanked the wheel and drove across the front yard of a neighbor's house and headed for a tree. At the last second she swerved back onto the street and continued to Mike's house at 40 miles per hour over the speed limit.

The way I saw it, I knew she wouldn't wreck that Mustang. She loved that car. And, I got to Mike's that much faster.

"Thanks, Mom," I said as I closed the door. "I'll call you tomorrow. I really appreciate it."

There was one evening when I was a teenager, living with my mom in the house in Cherry Crest, that exemplifies what an annoying child I was and how completely feeble my mother was at threatening me.

My friend Jerry from across the street and I were playing APBA Football, a board game. If I were to describe it, you would fall asleep, but playing it was a surprisingly fun time. Jerry and I were getting into it. It takes about three hours to finish and the trouble was we started a bit late in the evening. It was summer, so Jerry and I didn't need to get up the next day for school. My mother, on the other hand, had to work the next morning. She had gone to bed, so we turned down the music slightly and forged ahead into the second quarter. The game entails calling plays, shaking dice, and then looking up very realistic results off the player's cards and large cardboard charts. The dice shakers were yellow cardboard cylinders with metal bottoms that made a very satisfying and loud rattle that would add to the drama before spraying the dice out onto the table, with hopes of double sixes and a possible big play.

The music, our exhilaration and the rattling of those metal-bottomed dice shakers added up to a cacophony of sleep disrupting sounds. Aha! Not being completely insensitive, we figured out that if we turned up the heat, the furnace, that was housed right next to my mother's bedroom, would hum and growl and blow, thus blocking out our noisy play.

Perfect. Except for two small problems. Sometimes the double sixes would generate a whoop that was not masked by the white noise of the furnace. And second, as I mentioned before, it was summer. So a couple of hours of that furnace in August would make the house pretty hot. We were fine because we just opened the sliding door in the den that opened to the back yard. My poor mother, on the other hand, didn't have that luxury.

The furnace would stop. Then she would hear those shakers, wake up and come out of her room and into the hall, which was a straight shot through the house to the card table where Jerry and I were seated.

"What are you two doing? Keep it down. I need to get some sleep. Quiet. I am going back to bed."

I would turn up the thermostat a tad more. Flip the record, and on with the game.

The furnace would stop. Out she would come. "Will you two cut it out?"

"Sure, Mom. We're almost done. He'll be leaving in just a minute," I would lie.

This went on a number of rounds. Jerry, at one point, thought he better go so she could get some sleep.

"Are you crazy? It's just the start of the fourth quarter. She'll be fine."

She was back in the hall again. "Turn off that damn music. What is wrong with you? If you two don't stop playing that game . . . I don't know what I might do."

"Okay, Mom. Sorry. We're finishing up. Sit down, Jerry," I whispered, "She's fine. I have an idea." I went and got cotton balls and put them in the shakers. Voila! Less dramatic, but probably a smart move.

The game was almost over. It was tied. Revolving the dial on the furnace thermostat like a safecracker waiting to hear the last tumbler click, I turned up the heat one more notch. The furnace roared on. "Your turn, Jerry. Call your play."

The final minutes of our game were building to a fever pitch. We were whispering, but we were into it. I rolled a great roll, and unwittingly let out a whoop, because moments later Jerry was looking over my shoulder with his eyeballs jutting out in fear. I turned and looked down the hall.

My mother was standing in the hall in her zip-up, quilted housecoat. Her hair was stuck to her forehead and temples in sweaty, tight ringlets. Her arms were outstretched and they were quivering, slightly bobbing. She spoke very slowly. "Why . . . is . . . it . . . so . . . damn . . . hot? I am sweating. Did you turn up the heat? Did you turn up the heat to mask the noise? IT IS AUGUST! Are you out of your goddamned mind? Get . . . get . . . Go . . ." Her hands were shaking faster. Her head darted all around. Beside her in the hall was a small, narrow, high-back, antique chair. She grabbed it in both hands. "See this chair? This was my grandmother's chair. I love this chair. If you don't stop playing that game right this second I am going to smash this chair to bits." She held it up in front of her.

Jerry stood up.

"We are so close to being done, Mom. Jerry will leave in just a few minutes."

195

She set the chair down and lurched slowly towards us with her arms outstretched like the Mummy. "You . . . You . . . You . . . SLUT!"

"Huh?" I started to laugh.

"DON"T LAUGH AT ME!" she shrieked.

Holding my breath in an effort to stop laughing, I wheezed, "You called me a slut?"

Sounds started to come out of her mouth. They were not words. They didn't even resemble human sounds.

"Bye. Bye, Mrs. Castle. So sorry." Jerry scooted past her sideways and was out the front door.

My mother's vocal cords were able to reach still higher notes. In a shrill voice that should have broken our dishes, she squealed, "It was all I could think of. You . . . you . . . Ahhh. GO TO BED!"

"Man, we were almost finished. I can't believe you called me a slut. Sorry about the heat. Good night, Mom." She turned and with her shoulders slumped, dragged herself back down the hall.

"Oh, Mom."

She turned.

"Can I borrow the car tomorrow?"

"Of course. Good night."

# For Your Protection

Inherent in motherhood is the unconditional, uncontrollable, necessity to provide for the safety of their offspring. Keeping the kids safe is Job One. My mother is no different. It's just that sometimes her concept of safe doesn't necessarily line up with the norm.

I don't want to give the impression that my safety was ever in question with regards to my mother's care. For cripes sake, I knew she wasn't going to drive the Mustang into that tree on purpose at 50 miles an hour. She loved that car. And when she would be sick of my annoying behavior as a youngster, I knew she never meant it when she would yell, "Why don't you just go play on the freeway?"

There were the times when, though important, safety would take a back seat to anything exciting or fun. Living in the Midwest, tornado warnings were a common occurrence. Though, where we were, a bit north of Chicago, tornados actually striking were rare. But still, when the warnings would get especially serious, I would imagine that our friends and neighbors were probably following the advice.

When the warnings got really intense, my mother would take me outside to see how fascinating the weather was. It was wonderful. So quiet. The air was always perfectly still, and the sky had an eerie green hue to it. We'd be standing there, Mom and me, while neighbors were under a bed in the south-west corner of their house.

"Isn't it just beautiful, Cam? Look at the color of the sky. It is so still. Look at that tree. Not a leaf moving."

Well, we never got sucked away. And we never saw a tornado hit, but on the motherly, keepin' the kid safe scale, she was rather low. On the scale of showing me something really cool, she was at the top.

Like with fire.

If my mother ever heard sirens, she reacted like a track runner hearing a starting gun.

"Cammie, quick, it could be a fire. Here's your coat. Come on! Hurry, we'll miss it".

I remember vividly, being eight or so, getting tossed in the back of the car and racing down the street, catching up with the fire engine, and arriving at the fire right behind it. I can picture that house, engulfed in flames and the firemen working like crazy.

"Isn't this exciting, Cammie?"

I asked my mom recently about the fire engine chasing.

"My father loved taking us kids to see the fires. He would throw us in the car and race off to the fire. We did it all the time. Once, when I was babysitting for Kim's son, Brad, when he was little, and I heard a fire engine, I put him in the car, and we raced to the fire. When we got back and Kim was there, and I told her where we went, she got really mad. She didn't think a little kid should see such a thing."

"Not to mention the fact of driving a little kid you are watching *TO* a burning building." I added.

We used to have burglar drills.

I was sitting on the couch in the house on Arbor Lane, and watching TV. I was sixteen or so. My mother stood up from her chair.

"Cam. We are going to have a burglar drill. I have been thinking about this, and we need to be prepared. You can never be too prepared. I mean, if a burglar came to our door, we wouldn't know what to do. So, I have thought this out. Look at me. I am serious. Why are you smiling? Stop that. Now pay attention. This is what we are going to do. Stand up. Okay. No wait, sit back down. We need to practice like it is real. Okay. So we are watching TV, just like now, and a burglar comes to the door. You let him in. Get up. Good. Now go to the door and open it. You let him in, then . . . distract him. With a joke. You're funny, you can do it. Tell him a joke, so while you are distracting him, I do this."

Then she leapt out of her chair like a pouncing tiger and while running, said, "Then I run into the kitchen," and she is out of sight, then back in the living room, "and I grab the butcher knife." She is now holding a ten-inch long carving knife in the air. "Then I stab him in the chest. Like this." she said, while flailing and slashing the knife at the imaginary intruder. She stopped abruptly, then, completely composed, said, "There. See? It'll work. Do you know what you do? Can you remember? I am sure you can."

She then went back to the kitchen to put the knife in the drawer, returned, sat in her chair, sighed, and stared at the TV. I was still at the door, just looking at her.

"Oh, Johnny's on next. Why are you still standing there? Sit down."

We practiced that more than once.

Maybe safety wasn't on the front page, but if one of the children needed or really wanted something, she would go to any length to provide it.

"If there is something one of my kids need, there is nothing that is going to stop me from getting it for them. Nothing can stop me if I feel I have to get something done."

She said that to me recently. Then I started to think about it. Whether it was big or small, or, if you actually really wanted it or not, if she set her mind to it, it was going to happen. She would do anything for me. I have so many experiences to draw from, but one is such an absurdly, perfect example, it is all we really need.

She broke into a post office to send me hemorrhoid medicine.

It was a Friday night. I was a freshman, living in the dorms at Western Washington University, talking to my mom on the phone who was a hundred miles away.

"How are you, Cam?"

"Oh, fine."

"No, you're not. What's wrong?"

"Nothing."

"I can tell. Are you in pain?"

"Okay. I have a hemorrhoid. It is awful. I don't know what to do. It is so embarrassing."

"You poor thing. It isn't embarrassing. Everyone in our family has had them. Do you have Anusol?"

"No."

"Well, I need to get you some. I am going to get you some by tomorrow morning."

"Mom, it's eight o'clock on Friday night. How are you going to do that?"

"Don't worry about it. I'll take care of it."

The next day, at about eleven o'clock in the morning, I was sitting in my dorm room with my roommate Mike and a couple of friends. There was a knock on the door, and when I opened it, a mailman was standing there. On the landing on the fifth floor of the Beta dorms in Bellingham, Washington. He was holding a small box. "Here, this is for you." He handed it to me, turned, and left.

I sat down. I knew what it was.

"What is it?" My friends asked. "Open it."

There was no way I was going to open that box in front of them. I knew that even though my mother said she was going to send me hemorrhoid medicine at eight o'clock the night before, and there was no physical way she could have possibly done anything to have it delivered Saturday morning, I knew it was in there.

"Open it. What could it be? Delivered on Saturday. The guy brought it all the way up here. Aren't you curious?"

"Hey? Wanna smoke some pot?" asked Mike. He could tell I did not want to open that box, and once again, being the best roommate ever, distracted them.

After they left, I looked at the box and noticed there wasn't any postage. It just had my address on it.

I opened the little box and lifted out a tube of Anusol hemorrhoid medicine and held it up for Mike to see.

"Hmm," was his appropriate response.

I grabbed the phone and called my mom.

"How?"

"You got it? Great."

"How? How did you do that?"

"Well, I knew you needed it, so I broke into the post office last night and put it with the other mail."

"You, you . . . broke into the post office? How?"

"That's not important. It was easy. I am just glad you got it."

I have no idea how she did it. So many years later she remembers doing it but doesn't remember the specifics of committing that felony. All I know is, I talked to her on a Friday night, from a 100 miles away, and got hemorrhoid medicine handed to me on Saturday morning.

I never got sucked into a tornado or rear-ended a fire truck. I guess I knew, growing up with her as my mom, I was kind of living on the edge. But one other thing I have always known. She will do anything for me.

# My Mother and Catastrophes

Inherent in my mother's zest for life and uncontrollable spontaneity has been the potential for some mishaps. She is wildly impulsive during most waking hours. That fact has produced mountains of material regarding zany things she has attempted or acts that have had unpredictable results. When all is said and done though, after the dust has settled, there is usually something positive to be drawn from the ordeal.

Sometimes not.

My mother bought a new dining room set. She went all out. It was pecan, solidly built, with three removable leaves. There were six matching chairs. Less than one week after buying the set, she thought a dinner party was in order to show it off. Minutes before the guests were to arrive, as she was checking on the food and putting the finishing touches on her appearance, she decided a quick once over with wood cleaner would be just the ticket. She grabbed the yellow aerosol can with the brown top and sprayed a heavy dose of Pledge over half of the table.

"Boy, this stuff is effective. I don't remember it bubbling up before."

She looked more closely at the can. "Easy-Off Oven Cleaner."

"AHHH!"

The sulfuric acid oven cleaner was working and bubbling on the smooth lovely varnished finish of my mother's six-day-old pecan dining room table like the brew in a witch's cauldron.

On another occasion, before a particularly important date, my mother got her hair done at a different and very expensive salon. After spending a ridiculous amount of money on the wash and set, she came home with, believe it or not, a hairdo she liked. No need to fuss with it. Completely out of character, she didn't feel a need to change it. She found an outfit she was thrilled with. The house was clean. Everything was perfect.

"He will be here any minute. What else is left to do? I know."

She went into the bathroom, looked in the mirror. "I look good. Oh, just a little hairspray." She reached below the bathroom sink, opened the cabinet and grabbed the Final-Net. Squirt. Squirt. She lightly covered her hair. "That smells funny." She looked at the bottle. "Windex!! What kind of idiot would put the Windex in the bathroom?" She had to rinse out her hair, dry it like crazy and brush it out the best she could.

"Ding dong."

"Just a minute!"

The loudest scream I have ever heard, possibly the loudest scream ever uttered, came from my mother. We were getting ready to leave for the family party at my sister's house. She had been working long and hard on a Key-lime meringue pie. Crust from scratch, the filling just perfect. The last I saw before I left the kitchen to get something from my room was the meringue, fluffed up like angels had blown on it. It was lightly browned, fading to subtle beige before turning to snowy white chiffon slopes.

Then the scream. A blood-curdling wail. The sound that Edvard Munch heard in his head as he painted that distressful masterpiece would have sounded like the squeak of someone being sprayed with cold water compared to my mother's scream. I came running from my room. My mind couldn't grasp what might be around the corner in the kitchen.

My mother somehow had managed to drop her masterpiece upside down, under the bottom rack, meringue side down directly on the still red-glowing burner. It was smoldering. It was undulating. Delectable Key-lime filling was oozing over the hot burner in a futile attempt to escape. Like the lava flow of Mt. Vesuvius heading towards the city, the green substance kept moving.

My mother sat down on the kitchen floor and started to cry. It was a soft and quiet sound. It was mournful. The smell of burned limes and scalded cream hung in the air.

I turned off the oven.

# My Mother and Her
# Aversion to Authority

The third time my mother moved without telling me was a move to Forest Glade, a condo in Bellevue, Washington. Forest Glade? Come on. I know these things are named by a couple of guys with dice that have the words forest, glade, glen, park, view, river, dale, acres, arbor, crest, creek, and grand written on them.

"Hey, Al, come in here. We're naming the new subdivision. Okay, Ernie, roll 'em."

"Glen Glade!"

"Roll again."

The condo was fine. I didn't mind my room. There was a cabana with a kitchen, a ping-pong table and a Jacuzzi. There also was a pool with a diving board. This was before some moron killed himself slipping off a diving board, thus making every public and semi-public pool remove theirs so that another moron wouldn't kill himself using it. My question is: after they removed those boards in order to keep really stupid people safe, did folks stand on the chrome, upside down, u-shaped tube that supported the board, balance waveringly, and then try to dive from it past the two-and-a-half feet of composite rock in an effort to still dive into a pool? I know I did.

So before they removed it, my friends and I spent many joyful hours drinking alcohol and pushing each other off the end of the slippery diving board before they removed it for some silly safety reason.

The condo owners elected a board. The main problem with a board is that it exists. If a board is made up of people who:

A) Want to be on it.

B) Are retired.

you have a recipe for trouble. This board was both. They were inspired and had all the time in the world. The problem was there was really nothing for them to "Board" over. So they made rules. Lots of rules. Many, ever-changing rules. And seeing as everyone's ten-square-foot spot of beauty bark and two Rhododendrons were basically the same, they had to wield their will on the cabana and pool.

That's where my mother comes in. She hates rules. All her life she has had an aversion to authority. I love her for it. From drawing lines up the backs of her legs at her all-girls college to simulate the seams in the nylons she was ordered to wear, to tearing up the ridiculous and underserved ticket and throwing it in the judges face, my mother has always been defiant.

The board started proclaiming certain hours of pool use.

"Condo owners only hours."

"No children allowed hours."

"Retired, thrice-married couples who look repulsive in bathing suits only hours."

There was the, "Limited number of guests rule."

"No glass at the pool." Nothing to argue with there.

Then the one that set my mother off;. "No one may be at the pool unless the homeowner is present. AT ALL TIMES!"

That one was posted with the rest, on the corkboard next to the door of the Jacuzzi.

The reason these rules irritated my mother was that nobody ever used the pool. Most every resident was 65, out of shape, pale, and hated to swim. On an average day, less than one person would use the pool. On a sunny summer day, some of our family would come visit Grandma, and the kids would love swimming in the pool. But according to the new rules posted on the board, the melanoma-surviving matriarch of our family had to spend every moment beside the pool, in the sun, with her guests. She was not allowed to walk 27 feet past the rickety gate to her shaded patio for fear of breaking the rule.

The "no glass allowed" rule was reasonable, so my mother bought plastic wine glasses. One would not want to drink blush wine out of a plastic cup, for goodness sakes. So she found these very nice plastic, stemmed wine glasses.

We were by the pool one sunny afternoon, sipping wine, when the creaky pool door opened and two board members peered at us with tilted heads and squinty eyes. They were not in bathing suits, they where only there to check up on the people who were making noises that could possibly be sounds of people having fun. They huffed, turned abruptly, and slammed the green, mildew-highlighted door behind them with an "eeerg." (The rusty spring and mildewy latch didn't make for a very dramatic slam.)

The next day, posted on the board was a venomous note that warned if any condo-owner AGAIN was sighted at the pool with glass "they will be fined!"

Man, that pissed off my mother. She was incensed that they didn't just walk over and say, "You know you shouldn't have glass at the pool."

At which point she could have shown off her fancy and not inexpensive plastic stemware to the snobs. But no, they posted a threat. Bad move.

A few days later, on a wonderful, sunny, late afternoon, I wanted to go to the pool. My mother was home from work, tired and wanting only to relax in front of the TV. The last thing in the world she wanted to do was escort me out to the pool. Knowing that if I went by myself, and some board member saw me there without her, there would be another posting. So she begrudgingly followed me to the pool.

There was nobody in the pool, but at the one round table with a big umbrella at the far corner of the pool area, were seated all the board members. Seeing as it was such a lovely summer afternoon, they decided to have their meeting at poolside, a pool none of them had ever sunk their pasty white bodies into. But they were enjoying the surroundings nonetheless.

I went over to the opposite corner of the pool from them and flopped down on a chaise lounge to warm up in the sun. My mother stood at the edge of the pool and glared at the tittering group around the shaded table. The six self-righteous board members who were responsible for her standing in the sun in her dress and not sitting in her cool living room watching the news, were chattering away. She started to fume. I knew it right away, because I had seen her a-brewin' many times before. They all stopped their tittering and stared at my mother. She was wearing a very nice dress with a tasteful floral print and a belt. She had hose on and a pair of snappy new shoes from Nordstrom.

There was a long pause. They were quiet. She stared at them.

Then she dove, head first, in a perfect 9.5 swan dive into the pool. She swam the diagonal length of the pool and lifted herself out of the water at the ladder that was right next to the table. She stood up and shook her arms to her side to shake off some of the water. She gave her wet hair a sharp jerk to the right, adjusted her drenched dress and said, "Is that against the rules?"

Then she turned with a flourish, like a fifties Hollywood starlet, and walked past me. She stopped, turned to me and said, "Stay as long as you want," and went back to her condo to change, and finally watch the news.

You know what? Those board members never made a peep about me being alone at that pool.

Ever.

# Altered States

"**M**om, I don't remember you being at Northport for the family reunion that year," I said while peering at a framed photograph on my mother's wall.

"I wasn't."

"But you're . . . "

"I just cut out a picture of my head and put it between Bruce and Karin. It fit. I was mad I wasn't there. Makes me feel I was."

My mother changes everything. Anything she possesses, and many things she does not own, she has to alter. It is a sickness. That is not to say that sometimes it is not adorable and clever. Some of her alterations are remarkable, so long as they aren't done to any of your own precious heirlooms. But the fact is, she has to modify everything she can get her hands on.

Years before anyone heard of Photoshop, my mother mastered the art of changing photographs to fit her happy misperception of reality.

At a family party, my niece, my mom, and I were in the kitchen. On the refrigerator was a photo of my niece Abby.

Abby said, "That's weird. I remember that photo. But I have never had my hair that way."

My mom says, "Oh, that. I always thought your hair would look cuter that way. So I changed it."

"How?" Abby and I asked.

"Simple. I just cut out the background with scissors, trimmed your hair into that cute bob, then glued on a new background. I really think you should wear your hair that way. Don't you?"

Sometimes it is not so harmless.

My sister, Kim, paid a large sum to have an oil portrait painted of her, her husband Bruce, and their young boys, Brad and Drew. It turned out very well. Kim and Bruce were very pleased with it. A few days after it was hung above their fireplace, our mother came over to see it. Bruce was at work.

"What do you think, Mom?" my sister enthusiastically asked.

"Oh, it's very nice. Very. Hmm."

"What 'hmm?'" my sister stupidly asked.

"Well, I hate to say anything, but . . . it's Brad's lips. They are all wrong. He has beautiful Cupid bow lips. And those, they are thin and straight. I can fix that."

The problem is, our mother is very creative and talented. She has a remarkable artistic flair. So you never know if one of her harebrained schemes is going to end wonderfully or be a complete heart-breaking disaster.

Mom took the painting off the wall and fixed Brad's lips. Where there had been thin, straight lips, there was now a lovely, plump, turned-up-at-the edges, kisser. Very nice lips. The only problem was, they were a tad out of scale. Not to say he now looked like the Joker, but something had gone wrong. Big, out of proportion, full, puffy lips were beaming off of Brad's little face. My mom was very proud of her work, and my sister didn't know what to do, so they put the portrait back on the wall.

Bruce came home. Kim was in the kitchen.

"What the hell happened to Brad's lips!!!"

"What, dear?"

My mother watched my first daughter, Krissy, when she was an infant, so that my first wife and I could go out one evening. We had Krissy dressed in her cutest sleep-thing. It was soft flannel with an elephant on the front. The elephant had a little floppy ear with a small squeaker in it. It was adorable, and the little squeakie thing made Krissy smile every time we squeezed it.

When we got home, all was well. Krissy was asleep and my mom left. On the kitchen table was the ear of the elephant. My wife was horrified. She looked at that like she was watching some *National Geographic* documentary on the slaughter of African animals. Next to the severed cloth ear were three quarters taped together in a stack, and a note.

"Sleeping on that ridiculous thing would be like making the baby sleep on a stack of quarters. So I cut it off. Hope you don't mind. Krissy is wonderful. Love, Mom."

One of her alterations that has had the most lasting negative effect, say, 39 years and counting, occurred when she was watching Abby, my brother Truman's first child. Our mother went to visit them right after the birth. It was her first grandchild.

They foolishly went out and left Mom in charge. When they returned, not all was well. Abby was a little colicky and not sleeping. When my brother's wife, Candy, went to try to put Abby back to sleep, she noticed that Abby's T-shirt was hanging open. Candy had read that if you pull a t-shirt over the head of an infant, they relive the birth experience. So she bought the style that has two satin ties that cross in the front. My mother had cut those off.

"Why are the ties cut off Abby's shirt?" Candy called, trying to be heard over the baby's crying.

"Oh, I cut those off. They seem very uncomfortable. She was just lying on a knot. No child could sleep like that."

Candy harrumphed, and went to the drawer to grab another shirt. "The ties are cut off this one, too," she yelled.

"I cut off all of those silly ties. There is no way she could sleep with those. Just put her in a regular T-shirt. I couldn't find one"

Through clenched teeth that were making a grinding sound, Candy slowly hissed, "That is because I don't have any. Now what is she going to sleep in?"

"Oh," our mother pondered.

Planning ahead is as far removed from our mother's spontaneity as a drunk considering the next morning while ordering another drink.

One day I was sitting on the couch in my mother's condo. I was twenty. My sister, Kim, came over. She walked down the hall towards our mother's bedroom. The door was ajar.

"Mom? What are you doing?" she asked incredulously.

I turned my head, and very unfortunately, saw my mother through the open door. My 60-year-old mother was standing in front of her mirror holding a pair of scissors. Her left hand was holding the tip of the right cup of her bra. The left cup had no tip. Just a hole.

"Mom . . . Mom ? What . . . What?" my sister stuttered.

"Oh, this?" our mom replied. "The nipple look is in, but I need support. So I'm fixing my bras."

# My Mother Threw a Shoe Running to See Smarty Jones

Some families bond while camping or going on a long car trip together. Our family bonds in the emergency ward.

My father and his wife Mackie went through incredible and miraculous medical experiences. Between them they had four bouts of cancer, a stroke, and a number of mild and not so mild heart attacks. They survived all of that. They finally passed on due to infections or possibly just because their time had come. But while they were both baffling doctors and astounding nurses, my sister, brother, mother, assorted other family members and me, spent voluminous hours in hospital waiting rooms together passing the time.

We had witnessed so many wonderful successes from those two that we came to expect that, no matter how deathly serious the malady was, our loved one would most certainly pull through. So, those hours in the waiting room were not spent rubbing our temples in pre-grieving fear and flipping zombie-like through out-of-date copies of Newsweek and Redbook. No, we would talk. We would tell jokes. We would play games. Once I made a chessboard and chess pieces out of my business cards and a piece of yellow notebook paper, and my brother and I played a complete competitive game with it.

We would be in the waiting room while our loved one was having some incredible life saving surgery, and we would be laughing. Enjoying ourselves as best we could, and we would be bonding. Other folks coming and going from that waiting room would give us some pretty strange looks. We didn't care. Because in our confidence-inspired naiveté, we were making more than the most of a horrible situation.

Thankfully it had been a couple of years since a family medical disaster had taken place. Mostly through good luck, or because the elder matriarch, my mother, the most likely at age 84 to require some serious medical care, is as strong and feisty as a thoroughbred.

That was until . . .

My sister was throwing a wedding shower for my fiancée Laura. My mother was supplying the main dish, her famous sandwich loaf. This is quite an involved concoction. She cuts the crusts off a loaf of white bread, slices it lengthwise into five layers and then spreads cucumber slices, ham salad, egg salad and chicken salad each on a layer, stacks it up, and covers the whole thing in whipped cream cheese. It is always a hit, but for my 84 year old mother to produce that by herself in the little kitchen of her apartment in her fancy retirement home is no small order. But, of course she did it. She wrapped it up, got in her car and drove over to my sister's house. She parked way down the street, so as to leave spaces for the cars of the other ten women who would be arriving soon. This made perfect sense since my mother was the oldest one invited to the party and was bringing the food, so she, of course, parked the farthest away.

Thoughtfulness and wisdom sometimes just fly right past each other in opposite directions.

The shower was a huge success and everyone loved the sandwich loaf. Gifts were given, stories told. As the party was winding down and people were getting ready to leave, my mother stood up with a gasp and said with frantic urgency, "What time is it? Smarty Jones is running. It's the third leg of the Triple Crown! I have to see Smarty Jones! Have we missed it?"

"It's three o'clock, Mom." Kim answered. "I think it's on at three-thirty."

"Oh, I have just enough time to get home to watch him. Bye. Lovely party. Bye Laura. You look lovely. Bye, everyone." And she was out the door with a swoosh.

Kim was doing the dishes. Ladies were helping. Others were collecting their jackets when a neighbor lady from down the street ran into Kim's house and screamed, "Your mother has fallen!"

Kim dropped what was in her hands and, with the speed that Smarty Jones later would have wished he possessed, was out the door and down the street in a heartbeat.

On the street was our mother, wailing. Her face was scraped. There was blood on her white blouse. She was holding her side and moaning loudly. Nobody knew what happened.

"Mom. Mom. What happened? Are you hurt?"

"My chest. OW! My chest."

"Oh, my God! Which side, Mom? Which side hurts?"

"This side. Right here. It hurts here. OHHH!"

"That's your right side. Good. It's not your heart."

"I think I broke a rib. OHHH!"

By now all the ladies were in the street. It was a horrible and terrifying scene. Everyone's first thought was, "This is it!"

My mother was sprawled on the sidewalk and was in intense pain. Laura was crying. Emily, my nephew's wife, eight-and-a-half months pregnant, called 911. She was sobbing. My mother was moaning.

By now there were ten women in flowery spring dresses crying, and in what seems like forever, but was really about three minutes later, the ambulance arrived. My mother stopped moaning for a moment. She looked up at my sister, looked around at the surreal chaotic situation and asked, "Do you have a camera? Take a picture. Ow. I'm . . . ow . . . making a scrapbook for Cam and Laura's wedding. Take a picture."

The medics got her onto a stretcher and into the ambulance, and off it sped to the hospital.

The next day when Kim went to check on Mom, Mom said, "You didn't get a picture of me sprawled on the sidewalk with the ambulance and the fire engine, did you? It's okay. We can just go back and reenact it. I think it should be in the wedding photo album I'm making for them. Don't you?"

What happened was, as my mother was running down the street with a package under her arm, all the way to her car, in a frantic hurry to see Smarty Jones run in the Belmont, she slipped out of her very attractive backless, semi-high heeled, slip on, wooden soled shoe and tumbled forward in full force, breaking her fall with (and I quote her) "my right boob."

Actually she broke her fall, judging by her injuries, with her left hand, her right cheek and her chest. It was an awful crash, and she really is lucky she didn't knock out her front teeth or break a number of bones.

At the hospital my mom was rushed quickly into a room in the emergency ward. This was obviously a pretty well funded hospital, that fact given away by the very nice TV in each of the emergency rooms. Your own TV. Which to me, proves that when they say, "We will check you out and try to get you out of here as fast as we can," they are lying through their masks. Because obviously The Board voted to spend all that money on TVs in the emergency rooms because they know that they are going to leave anyone who is unlucky enough to find themselves there, hours longer than necessary for (and I have done hundreds of hours of research on this) NO REASON AT ALL!

My mother was in her room, and as they were carefully slipping her out of her clothes and into a gown and hooking her up to the machines to monitor everything, she looked over the shoulder of the nurse and said, "Hey. Is that a TV? What time is it?" Looking at the clock next to the TV, she said, "It's three-forty! The race is on! Turn it on. Turn it on. I want to see Smarty Jones. He's running right now."

So the nurse, later to be the enormously unaccommodating nurse, stopped what she was doing and turned on the TV.

The race was just starting. So they watched it. My mother got to see the race after all. Smarty Jones was leading the whole way, up until the end. But he lost by a length. The camera showed the horse's owner in the box seats in his wheelchair, with oxygen tubes in his nose, and they mentioned the 50 million dollars that he was not going to get because his horse did not win the Triple Crown, and the nurse resumed hooking my mom up to the machines.

Oh . . . by the way, my mother has never before, as far as any of us siblings know, ever been the least bit interested in horse racing. But, none of us even ask the question. Not even days later. "Smarty Jones? Mom? I didn't know you were into horse racing."

That is because we grew up with her and her unbelievable spontaneous enthusiasm that you can only appreciate and never fully understand.

An example would be a phone call I had with my mother a few years earlier.

"Hi mom. How's it goin'?"

"I can't talk now. The Mariners are on."

"Huh? The Mariners? You hate baseball."

"Gotta go. Ichiro is up! Talk to you later. Bye."

"Mom? Mom?"

She was nuts over that horse, and we didn't give it another thought.

While Laura was at the shower and my mother was crashing, I was busy running all over the place with my sons, Mason and Max. I walked in the house after picking up my son, Mason, from where he was taking his

SATs and dropped him off at his high school so he could catch a ride to Portland to play in a two day basketball tournament. I then picked up my other son, Max, after getting talked into buying him yet an even bigger fish tank for his goldfish, with all the accessories, on his promise that his next seven allowances, that he usually doesn't earn, are going right back to me. In my arms was his tank. Hopping up and down with joy, Max said, "Let's set it up. Let's set it up." Then the phone rang.

"Hello."

"Cam? It's Laura. Your mom . . . *zzzcrtzz* . . . has . . . *crrrzzztttzz* (sobbing) you need to *zzzzccrdzzz* . . . my signal is not very . . . *cccrdzzdck.*"

"What? What? You are cutting out."

"You need to go to Mountain View . . . *zzzxxxcrrrdzkkzz.*"

"Huh?

"Mountain View Hospital! (Sobbing) She has fallen. You need to . . . *zzzxxxccrkk...*"

I believe because the cell phone signals pass through the cosmos to go up and get back down to us, gives some higher being with a nasty flair for mischief, the chance to pick out those most important calls and mess with them. Have you ever been talking to someone on your cell phone that you just didn't want to talk to for another second, yet the call goes on and on? Has that call ever cut out? No. But if you ever have a call containing the words "emergency ward," I guarantee you the next sound you will hear on your cell phone will be "*zzzxxxcrttyzzx.*"

I hung up. The phone rang again.

"Yeah?"

"Me again. Sorry. I had no signal. Your mother has fallen. You need to go to Mountain View Hospital. Wait. Here's Kim."

"Cam?"

"Yes."

"Can you do something for me?"

"Yes. Yes, of course. What?"

"Mom wanted me to tape the horse race for her. I just can't make it work. Oh, my. If you could just . . ."

"No problem."

My mother was, at that moment, in an ambulance being raced to the hospital. I didn't really know what was wrong with her, but it sounded very serious. So it was time to snap back into that medical crisis frame of mind that seemed like only a short time ago, was a constant in our lives.

I ran to the TV, grabbed a tape, found the right channel and pressed record. *Hmm. The race was about to start. She will want to know how it turned out. I better watch it. Man it takes a long time to load those horses into that starting thing.*

"And they're off!"

"Cloppity, cloppity, cloppity . . ."

*He lost?*

*Oh, shit! She's gonna be mad.*

As I walked into the hospital, I passed two incredible salt-water fish tanks that would make Jacques Cousteau proud and went to the reception desk at the emergency ward. To enter the area where the patients are, you need to go through the large, secured electronically activated door. One of the two nurses at the reception desk have to see you at the door, recognize that you are someone who should enter, and reach over and press the button on the wall around the corner from their desk, thus emitting a very loud buzzer sound as the big door slowly opens. I entered and was pointed to the first room on the right.

I pulled back the curtain and went in. Mom was sitting up in the bed and looked great. Kim was standing beside her and they both looked . . . happy. Kim and Mom were thrilled that I was there because we all knew the drill. We were going to be there a very long time, and we were going to make each other laugh. All of our family members are pretty darn funny, but in crunch time, humor crunch time, like, let's say being in the emergency room with your severely damaged 84 year old mother, that kind of crunch time, I am supposed to be . . . funny. And I was. And Kim was. And Mom was pitching in. The trouble was that the reason we were there was because Mom most likely had a BROKEN RIB!

So, it was funny joke. "Ahhh!" Funny joke, "Owww." Funny joke. "Ewww."

Mom was laughing, and then pushing her hand against her right ribcage, grimacing, pausing for half a second, and then, with bright happy eyes, picking the conversation up right where it had stopped.

We were having fun and time was passing. Those passing by the curtain surely thought we were nuts.

I looked at the clock and realized it was an hour and a half since Mom had been admitted.

I peeked out past the curtain and saw the nurse, the Belmont savvy nurse, who was filling out forms with an intense grimace.

"Kim, I haven't even asked. What's the program here? What's next? What are we waiting for?"

"The x-ray. They are going to give her an x-ray to see if her rib is broken or not."

"It's been an hour and a half. I'm gonna ask."

"Be careful. She's not very friendly."

"Okay."

I stepped past the curtain and three feet into the hall. My mother's room was right across from the nurse's station. I stood there feigning sheepishness waiting to make eye contact. No luck. There were two nurses both intensely typing out info and filling out forms.

I cleared my throat. "Ah. Ah." They didn't look up. They were four feet away and knew I was beckoning, but nothing. "Ah, excuse me . . . ahhh."

One looked up SO bothered. "What?"

"Ah . . . I showed up late and ah . . . don't really know the program . . . I mean . . . what's next?"

"Don't stand there and talk to me," she snapped. "This area . . . this area is . . . you cannot talk to me here. I will see you in the room. This is a patient confidentiality area. And you cannot talk to me here. Go into the room and I will be there in a moment. We are very busy."

"Patient confidentiality area? What the hell does that mean? Am I going to give away some secrets? 'My mom fell on her boob!' Or am I going to obtain some big time secrets from the other patients? 'Oh looky here. On this chart. Mrs. Johnson has a thrombose hemorrhoid! WOO WEE!' Boy, you're right. Better keep these three feet of hallway off limits to your unseemly patient visitors because you never know if they might have Superman eyesight and work for the National Enquirer. And, they are so starved for news that they might need to print the earth shattering stories that are contained on your hand scribbled notes on those forms on your desk."

I didn't say any of that.

The nurse finally came in to Mom's room. As she walked past me and went to our mother, she transformed into this sickenly phony, fawning, young Mother Teresa. She spoke sweetly to our mother and fluffed her pillow.

I asked, "I was wondering how long it will be until . . ."

"X-rays, they take an hour. It takes an hour."

Timidly, I started to say, "Well, we have been here an hour and a- . . ."

"They take an hour. That is what I say. I always say that. It doesn't mean I know how long it takes. I just always say an hour," the nurse snapped.

"Right. Well, we have already been here an hour and a- . . ."

"It will be an hour," she growled.

"Another hour?"

"I said it takes an hour to get an x-ray. That is what I say. Look, there could be ten patients ahead of you. There could be people dying. There could be people failing. Look at your mother. She is not failing. Is she? If we had people failing, we would take care of them first. Don't you think that is the way it should be?"

"Yes, of course. But ah . . . are there . . . I mean . . . ah . . . but we have already been here an hour and a – half. Do you know when they might take her x-...?

"I'll check." She turned and punched the curtain out of the way, and was gone.

Kim said, "See."

About forty-five minutes later, a nice girl came in and wheeled our mom off for the x-ray.

My sister Kim, who has put forth the most effort in all of our family emergencies, one who has put forth truly Herculean effort in our family emergencies, said, "I'm supposed to be at a dinner party."

I made her go. The hard part was over. I was thinking it would just be: get the x-ray, have the doctor tell us what it is, and hopefully take Mom home.

"I'll call you on your cell phone as soon as we find out. Go. But if I call you and you have a full signal and you hear, *zzchxxxvcvvtyyxz*, come back."

About twenty minutes later, they brought my mom back. A few minutes after that, miraculously, the doctor came bursting through the curtain and into her room. I say miraculously, because we had been here for three hours, and we were in room "One," right next to the hub of activity, right next to the forbidden alter of "Patient Confidentiality," and we had yet to set eyes on a doctor. I was sure this doctor had been performing miracles just outside of the reach of our senses. But mostly all my senses had picked up to that point was the aura of bitchy nurses, the sounds of the Stanley Cup hockey game, the sight of those really cool fish tanks, and the smell of my awful, yet incredibly efficiently dispensed cup of vending machine coffee. But here, finally, was the Doctor.

There is nothing more comforting than finally having, tending to you hurt loved one, after so long of a wait, the Doctor. *Share with us. Make it better. What is it? And what do we do?*

The Doctor said, "So the x-ray didn't show us much. Didn't think it would. You see, the part of her ribs where she hurt herself is mostly cartilage, and that doesn't show up on the x-ray. So it might be broken, but it most likely is just cracked. Like a twig you know. Like this. (He made a gesture like breaking a stick.) So what we do with a rib like that is not wrap it. We want the lung to be able to breathe unimpeded, and for the rib to heal itself. So I will prescribe some pain medication and in time, oh, I'd say two to four weeks, you will start to feel better."

"Great," I replied. "One question. So Doctor, if her rib was broken what would you do?"

"Oh, if it was broken, what we would do is not wrap it, because we would want the lung to breathe freely, and that would allow the bone to heal by itself. So I will write you the prescription. Take care." He was out of the room past that curtain like a puff of smoke.

"He is nice" said Mom, as the Vicodin that the nurse finally gave her before she went off to the x-ray kicked in.

I was thinking that we had just spent three hours there, and we were not out yet. We had been waiting for an x-ray, and a doctor's diagnosis, and what it all turned out to be was this:

If your rib is bruised or cracked, we don't wrap it.

If it is broken, however, we don't wrap it.

But before we decide which to do, we need an x-ray.

Now the x-ray, though vitally important, won't tell us if the rib is broken or bruised because the area of ribs that are being x-rayed are mostly cartilage and don't show up on the x-ray.

What the hell?

They should have just had the receptionist poke her in the ribs, and if she screamed, give her a Vicodin and tell her to get back in the car?

The nurse came in and said, "I will fill out the discharge forms. You can get dressed." She left.

"Okay, Mom, we can go."

After trying to figure out who should dress her, Mom struggled out of the bed for the first time and realized she should use the rest room. She walked very slowly at first and then gathered her footing and went out past the curtain. The nurse led her in the right direction. I watched her walk.

As she was walking away to the bathroom, holding the gown closed behind her with her left hand, she was walking in a certain way. She was walking with style. Honestly. Even in that gown, in pain, in the emergency ward, and with that bitchy nurse beside her, she was walking with an air of style. Her upper body was tilted slightly to the left. Her right arm was away from her body. Her four fingers of her right hand were pointed out and away from her. She has a stylish walk and I saw it. It was not forced. It was not comical. It was not affected. It was a walk of someone who has such class and style, such unassuming, unaffected class and style, that even walking in a hospital gown with intermittent substantial jabs of pain, her natural elegance showed through. I was quite taken by that image.

I went out to get the car and drove it to the front. I went through the large secure door again. I had been through that door at least seven times to either use my cell phone or go get a cup of that horrible coffee.

To get back in, remember, I had to be let in by one of the girls at the receptionist's desk. The ridiculous system to get through that door went like this. Stand by the door. If one of the girls looked up and noticed, they then had to press a button, which was conveniently positioned around the corner in a room behind them. I learned right off the bat that it was completely inappropriate to try to get the ladies attention by clearing one's throat, coughing, or God forbid, saying "hey!"

So, I stood there, like so many times previously, and shuffled my feet and sighed.

Finally, after both girls convinced the other it was not their job to press the button, one, with a big "harrumph" slid her chair back, reached into the room behind her, and punched the button.

The very loud buzzer, the slow opening door, and I was back in the exquisitely decked out emergency ward. I walked past the sneering nurses whose annoyance seemed to grow each time that crazy-loud door buzzer went off, and returned to my battered and Vicodin-soothed mother.

After watching those nurses for three and a half hours, if I had to rate them on their, so called, bedside manner skills, I would have said (and it probably wasn't their fault), filling out the forms was so much more important to them than anything that might have been important to the patients or their loved ones.

I wondered if there was a form to fill out to explain why a patient died while you were filling out a form?

Mom had dressed herself, and I walked her to the car. I got her very delicately into the passenger seat. She was sitting there with her prescription in her hand, and I thought, "Wait a minute. It's late. She only needs one more pill for tonight. She needs to get to bed.

Rather than make her wait while I find a pharmacy and wait for them to fill the prescription, I'll just run in there and ask the 'accommodating' nurses, or the vaporous doctor for just one pill to get her through the night. I can't believe I didn't ask before we walked out."

I went back to the door. I struck my pose, again. I was sheepish and sweet like the porcelain Boy in Blue. They looked up. They looked at each other like parents going through a child custody battle, and the loser reached all the way around the wall and punched the button. The loud buzzer went off. The door slowly opened.

"Hi. You probably thought you were rid of me. Ha ha. Ah . . . it's kinda late and I think I should get her to bed. Could she have just one of those pain pills, and then I could fill her prescription tomorrow?"

I think she misheard me and thought I said, "I'm a strung out heroin addict and can I have a dozen of those or something maybe way stronger? And a syringe and a rubber tube. I'm okay to drive, and she's just fine. I threw her in the back under a blanket. Oh, and you are ugly! And you suck!"

At least I was guessing that was what I thought she thought I said, judging by her response.

"NO! We do not dispense medicine here. We only give medicine here. If you are a patient, we can give you medicine. But we cannot just give you medicine. Do you get it? If you are a patient we can give it to you. But we cannot dispense it. I will get you a list of all-night pharmacies. Here."

" . . . "

"I'm sorry. But I cannot dispense medicine to you. Do you understand?"

" . . . "

"Do you understand?"

I finally made myself speak, "She's only fifteen feet from here. She's right there. You can see her. Do you need me to carry her back in here?"

"NO! We do not dispense medicine! That is what the pharmacies are for. I cannot help you. I am very busy. We have rules. Lots of rules. I don't make them. I cannot give you any medicine." Then she spun away from me and stalked off. With her head tilted upward with an air of determination, she swiftly headed off down the hall to either care for a patient or snap at yet another annoying family member that was basically just in her way.

I went out and got in the car. My mother looked at me to see what I got for her potential nighttime pain, and I gave her the piece of paper.

"Here ya go."

"They wouldn't give you one pill?"

"Nope."

"Those nurses were nice though, weren't they?"

Okay, so the Vicodin was still working.

I took her home. She lives in a wonderful retirement home. Her apartment is decorated beautifully and has a very comfortable feel. She was happy to just take some Tylenol for the night. She assured me she was okay and looking forward to having a small medley of egg, ham and chicken salads that most likely would be served on just the crust of some very fine bread.

I got in my car, leaned back, and let out a deep sigh. Yet another emergency ward experience, and everyone was okay. I thought to myself, "Mom's gonna be all right. I will be home soon for a late dinner with Laura. I bet

Max has that fish tank gurgling just perfectly. Mason's playing basketball. Kim is at her dinner party. But I am more than a tad worried about Smarty Jones's owner."

# Dancing in the Kitchen

**M**y mother went to a doctor the other day.

"Hello, Mrs. Udovic. I am Dr. Miller. What brings you to me today?

"I haven't been to a doctor in a while and thought it would be a good idea."

"Okay, Mrs. Udovic. Let's start with how old you are."

"I am 93."

"Ha. You mean 73.'

"No. 93."

"Oh, my. Well, you are in excellent shape for your age. Let's start. Can you give me a list of the medications you are taking?"

"Yes, I can. (deep breath) I take a multiple vitamin every morning and sometimes a Tylenol."

"No, I mean your *list* of medications."

"I don't have a list. I don't take any."

"My goodness, Mrs. Udovic. I have to ask, to what do you attribute your great health?"

"That's easy. I am always happy."

So that is why, a bit of time after that, I was very upset to get this call.

"Hi, Mom. How are you?"

"Not well. I am so upset that Steve won't call me."

"Well, he's busy and he has often gone a long time without calling you."

"This time it's different. It's been so long. You know it goes back to . . ."

She went on to describe a big suitcase full of issues that has followed my mother and Steve on their journey together through this world. My mother's relationship with my brother Steve has been more dramatic than most and could easily be a book all in itself. Add to that our mother's ability to make the most mundane things as volatile or exciting as a bomb or county fair, and you have the recipe for some emotionally rocky interaction. After she finished with her thoughts, worries, and regrets brought on by the lack of calls, she said this:

"I don't dance in the kitchen or have happy attacks anymore."

That sentence hit me like a ton of bricks. I pictured her, at the age of 93, dancing by herself in her little kitchen. Then memories came rushing in and I realized at that moment that "happy attacks" are the secret. Happy attacks are the Rosetta stone for how she has managed to survive the massive amount of hardship she has endured in her life then be able to say to the Doctor, "I am always happy."

Happy attacks. I can't explain them or understand where they come from, but if it could be bottled . . . I can't imagine.

Just a few days after that call I got another call.

"Hi, Cam. Good news. Steve called me, and you won't believe this. I was completely wrong. None of my crazy reasons for why he didn't call were true. He was just busy. It is all better now."

"That's great, Mom."

"Yes, it is. Oh, and I'm dancing in my kitchen again."

# Conclusion

So, there you have it. My mother is crazier than your mother. But in all of her craziness my life never was forced to take a turn for the worst. Her zany antics either led my life off in a better direction, or at the very least taught me to look at everyday life in a specific way. That is to first view this kaleidoscope image of reality that is swirling around us with a positive attitude. Look for the joy and happiness in every instance first. And if after looking, you find instead that in some instances what you really have is a big load of crap, look immediately for the humor surrounding or contained within that bit of crap.

I have managed to keep my psyche moderately intact through the anguishes of some parts of this ride of life by reminding myself, this isn't a tragedy, it is the makings for a really good story. This isn't a bout of bad luck, but a humorous adventure disguised.

I thank my mother and my father every day for instilling in me the perspective through which I unconsciously view the world. Yes, Mom moved three times without telling me, but my life improved with each of those moves. And you could look at her crashing and burning while darting out of Laura's bridal shower as foolish and disruptive. But, what it showed everybody was that the fountain of youth is found in spontaneity. And it also showed that my mother, like my father, was able to find strength through adversity with humor. As she was lying on the street hurting and bleeding, her first thought was honestly, "take a picture for the wedding album!"

This book has only scratched the surface of the wealth of crazy antics my mother has performed. I need only to clear my head for one second, and I can retrieve another example. Let's see. Yes. My mother and father were driving to a cocktail party. Behind them was another car of some friends who were following because, supposedly, only my mother knew the way. After a short time, my Mom realized there was no way in hell she was going to find the place. So she pulled over, with the friends behind, went to a payphone and called a cab. Within minutes a cab showed up. She went to the driver's window and handed him the address of the party on a piece of paper and asked him if he knew where it was. He said, "Sure. Hop in." She said, "Nope. We'll follow you." And with that, she got in her car and they all followed the empty cab to the party.

She and I lived together, just the two of us, for many years. Those years molded me into what I am today. I don't know what I am today, but I do know that whenever anybody reads any of these stories, they then look at me and say, "Well, that explains it."

Then I ask," What? Explains what?"

And they say, "Nothing."

I also have never quite been able to right my financial ship after the large amounts of water it took on early with the routinely fiscal logic of my mother that entailed, as I have mentioned earlier, "Hmm. No money. No groceries. Hey, let's go out to dinner! I'll write a check. If we're going, let's go somewhere nice."

So I have been bailing out my fiscal frigate ever since, but I have survived somehow to stay out of the poor house. And though the size of my IRA is nowhere near the size of my memory bank filled with happy remembrances, I can only thank my mom from the bottom of my heart for her being just who she is and what it has meant to me.

Thank you, Mom.
Love, Cam.

My mother insisted (demanded) that this picture be in the book. So here it is. My girlfriend I renamed Hannah took this picture of me in Seattle after the drive across the country in 1974. My mother feels that all of her antics couldn't be too damaging if I can look as happy as that.

# Acknowledgements

I first want to lovingly thank my beautiful wife Laura for her unwavering support and guidance, without which this book could not have possibly been published. My daughter Krissy helped immensely with the first round of editing. Susan Jensen then worked tirelessly to professionally edit this book. Any grammatical errors are not due to any lack of her amazing talents but are a result of my stubbornness. Sometimes jokes just aren't grammatical. I want to thank my Whidbey Island writers group for all of their fabulous insight and advice. I am so proud of my five children, Krissy, Mason, Max, Carter and Wilson who are all just magnificent. And finally, I want to thank my mom. It has been a crazy ride with her at the wheel. But it was never dull. Love ya, Mom.

Made in the USA
Middletown, DE
04 December 2023

44610682R00154